THE PLACE OF TRUST

THE PLACE
OF TRUST

MARTIN LUTHER
On the Sermon on the Mount

Edited by Martin E. Marty

1817

Harper & Row, Publishers, San Francisco
Cambridge, Hagerstown, New York, Philadelphia
London, Mexico City, São Paulo, Sydney

The Luther text in this book is from *Luther's Works,* Volume 21 (translated by Jaroslav Pelikan), © 1956 by Concordia Publishing House, St. Louis, Missouri. Used by permission.

FIRST EDITION

Designer: Jim Mennick

Library of Congress Cataloging in Publication Data

Luther, Martin, 1483–1546.
   THE PLACE OF TRUST.

   Contents: Do not be anxious—When you pray—Blessed are.
   1. Sermon on the mount.   I. Marty, Martin E., date.   II. Title.
BT380.L79   1983   226'.906   83–47727
ISBN 0–06–065449–X

83 84 85 86 87 10 9 8 7 6 5 4 3 2 1

To Sylvia and Jaroslav Pelikan
in trust

CONTENTS

INTRODUCTION

By Martin E. Marty

Trust is at the root of healthy human life. Psychologist Erik Erikson speaks of "basic trust" as the most profound need and outlook. The child, dependent upon elders, grows in confidence to the degree that parents and others provide reasons for trust. We base our marriages on ways of life that extend the wedding vows, which promise trust. Where trust is stretched we prop it up with contracts, documents that make possible some security. Where trust breaks down there can be no mental health. Paranoia, for example, is precisely the inability to extend trust, perhaps because its victim has not felt trust.

Trust is also at the root of healthy spiritual growth. Philosopher Gabriel Marcel relates trust to belief in someone. "To believe in someone," which means "to place confidence in him, is to say, 'I am sure that you will not betray my hope, that you will respond to it, that you will fulfill it.' " To feel confident enough to say that and to have reasons for meaning it is close to the heart of what Christians call faith. They may flesh out the idea of faith by connecting it with contents: "I believe *that* God made me, that Christ saves me. . . ." Yet such understandings of faith are hollow unless they are grounded in the rich notion of trust: "I believe *in* the God who made me, the Christ who saves me. . . ."

People who are sure of their "belief that" may not be spiritually profound or psychologically healthy. They are busy measuring how much of such belief others have, and whether they have the contents, called doctrines, exactly correct. People who have reasons to be sure of their "belief in" can be freed of such concerns, free to accept what each day brings, to extend trust to others, and to grow in trustworthiness. Anything that contributes to this sense of trust, then, contributes to wholeness and wellbeing.

Trust does not come as a package deal off which one lives the rest of life. The child may display it in most pure form. That is why Jesus of Nazareth is pictured as using the child for a model of faith. Yet, as the child moves through the passages of life, one form of faith will fade. It must be replaced by other forms suited to other stages and new unfoldings of personality. On a death bed one may rely on a trust as simple as that of the child. Yet to move toward death saying to an unseen God, "I am sure that you will not betray my hope, that you will respond to it, that you will fulfill it," is to speak against the background of many trials and tests.

The aged person who trusts, reviews a life in the light of a God who often seemed absent. Where were you, God, when I lost my job for no good reason in hard times? What were you doing to win my trust when you let one son be killed in a plotless war and another drift away in the drug culture? Why should I trust you, God, when you seemed silent and remote as I fought off alcoholic addiction? My spouse turned out not to be trustworthy despite his vows made in your name. Where was trust? What did your name mean? And now I am separated from my family in this intensive care ward. I cannot trust what tomorrow will bring; must I trust only the life-support systems?

Astonishingly, it is when such questions come that most believers find that trust, tested, endures. Yet to move between the trust of the child and the trust of one at the point of death is to walk on a path that offers daily challenges and opportunities, each of which calls forth trust. We can speak of the place of trust as a way of envisioning support for the journey of life.

This little book is a kind of road map for that

journey, and its author is a well-recognized guide. Martin Luther, sixteenth-century Reformer of the church catholic, spent his life in a struggle for faith. He would let nothing stand between a God he found to be, in the end, trustworthy, and his threatened human existence. No church laws or systems were strong enough to support him. No achievement of his personal life was sufficiently reliable for him to base trust on it.

Instead, Martin Luther taught himself, and retaught elements of the church, how to trust. For him this did not mean spiritual calisthenics in which he would make charts of improvement. Rather, he let everything depend upon the character of God as revealed in the sacred scriptures and in the spoken word of or about Jesus, who disclosed that trustworthy character of God.

Whoever has read those scriptures, especially the Gospels in which the words and works of Jesus are the subject, knows that the Sermon on the Mount in Matthew chapters five to seven is the most clear call for trust and the most painstaking—if also starkly dramatic—prescription for how to come to trust, how to grow in trust. To come across pages by Martin Luther setting forth some meanings of these trust-proclamations is to find new ideas for the walk along the path to the place of trust.

As I introduce these pages, I remind myself that

although many have read *about* Luther, most have not read Luther. The idea of reading about Luther prepares one for pages of heavy theological writing. Were not his struggles devoted to words and concepts we do not often use today, words like "indulgences," and "justification"? Whoever knows anything about theologians knows that they tend to use difficult and often private language.

Surprise awaits those who approach Luther looking for hard ideas in hard language. He can deal with the profound notions on which we place wagers about the future, notions of faith and trust, in terms that a child can grasp. On the pages that follow, for instance, we hear him going on at some length about the way birds in their singing are the real theologians! Here is a love of nature, a gentle spirit that belies the often stormy and sometimes even nasty controversialist of Christian history.

Few readers of this book will find the biblical passages on which Luther commented to be unfamiliar. I have chosen sections in which Jesus urges us to "be not anxious," and linked them to his advice about how to pray in the form of the Lord's Prayer and to the Beatitudes, the "Blessed are . . ." pages. Few lines of scripture have appeared on more wall mottoes or samplers, been memorized in more Sunday School rooms, or cherished by more people of faith than these. Yet, for that reason, their features can easily wear smooth and their outlines disappear. The texts lose some of their power to shape us.

In order to uncover fresh meanings, then, we listen to the way a person who has experienced both the absence and presence of trust sets them forth. Luther's is not the only way, not necessarily the best way. In some respects, we live further from his world of sixteenth-century Germany than we do from the world in which Jesus first spoke these words. Yet even where Luther's world upsets and jars us, his writings serve to remind us of how urgent it is to apply the language of trust to the circumstances of another time and place—*our* time and place. To know that people pursued trust in the first and sixteenth centuries is interesting to each of us as historians. To learn from them some ways to do the pursuing in our time is the reason why we pursue the literature of devotion.

I have chosen not to prepare an anthology, a "Book of Quotations," which might raid writings from the 110 huge volumes the German publishers of Luther have been issuing for over one hundred years. Such selecting is an attractive idea, since Luther expressed himself so vividly that thousands of his lines make their way into books of quotations. The problem with such an approach, however, is that you can make a complex figure say almost anything, but you cannot be sure you are following his thought reliably. For that reason I have decided to reproduce sustained passages from his comment on three chapters of Matthew.

I have chosen to call this book of Luther on the Sermon on the Mount *The Place of Trust.* The book speaks of "the place of trust" in a double sense. On the one hand, it implies that there is a place for trust in the Christian life. On the other, we conceive of trust as a kind of place to which we aspire. We approach it as if on a journey, following a path. These pages invite the reader to pursue the path on the way to the place; they do not always provide the path, at least not in any simple sense. That is because neither the Gospel nor Luther in his comments can close our minds to some nagging thoughts. Thus you may read Luther on Jesus telling how God cares for the birds, which do not fall to the ground without God knowing. Yet birds *do* fall, so the ending is not simply happy. What does it mean to trust a God even though and when the creatures—and I am one of them—"fall to the ground"?

A grand clue is to see how Luther focuses on the centrality of a trustworthy God who beckons trust in every circumstance. Philip Watson summarized Luther's thought in the book title *Let God Be God.* Letting God be God will not necessarily fatten bank accounts, keep hair from falling or birds from dying. It will help put a fresh perspective on the days along the path. Try this: when dark thoughts obscure a day, ask yourself, in the light of the "be not anxious" pages here: "Are these thoughts about today? Or do they reflect guilt from yesterday or worry about tomorrow?" Almost always they will be looking backward or forward beyond the day. Yet if God is in control, then *this* day looks different. If the God who sent Jesus and who vindicated Jesus' death by raising him, the God of Christian faith, lives and is in control, then forgiveness for the past is available and fear for the future unnecessary. This is a message Luther opens up for the patient reader.

The patient reader, however, grows impatient. He or she wants to know what to *do* to increase this sense of contact with a trustworthy God who controls this day. For that reason, in this rearrangement I have then relocated the language about prayer, in which Luther, expounding Jesus, gives some rather precise direction about what to "do." This does not mean that he offers techniques. He spends little time describing postures or prescribing language. He gives lessons on short prayers, mere thoughts, quick conversational wrestling bouts with God, all with an interest in the character of the trustworthy God.

A third chapter relocates from the beginning of the Sermon on the Mount to the end the Beatitudes. They picture something of the way the trusting life looks, and how God looks at the trusting life. Here as always the accent is not on what my disciplines achieve, but on who God is and how God acts in blessing us.

It has been necessary to condense these pages somewhat to eliminate repetition. It would be cheating to pretend that Luther says all the right things about Jews, the Catholicism of his day, or the people around him. It would be unfair to suggest that his language was always polite and polished, that he never talked crudely about "bellies" and bodies as "bags of worms." So I have left some of his upsetting passages intact so that we can be sure we are confronting the real, fallible Luther. Yet, if such lines appeared constantly, they would distract from the purpose of this book as a map for our own paths; thus many of the places marked with ellipses [. . .] included an oversupply of such sixteenth-century references. I have also removed footnotes in which the translator, my own teacher and friend Jaroslav J. Pelikan, explains his choice of terms in difficult passages. Those explanations, important for scholars, need not hold our attention or distract us in our present pursuit.

To satisfy the scholarly impulse in every reader,

however, I should mention that we are not sure that Luther spoke every word exactly as recorded here. Some scholars are suspicious of the hearing and writing of his students who took notes on his sermons. Were they completely accurate? Yet certainly the drift of Luther is here, for often in his sermons to congregations, which is what these paragraphs once were, he revealed most clearly what his life and faith were about.

This is not a book, then, for historical critics who want to know everything about Luther's world, or literary critics who want to discuss everything about Luther's writing, though all of us have historical and literary sides to which these passages will appeal. We come to it not as critics, but as people in search of the place of trust. Today we are learning from scholars how to use texts as means of disclosing a world we would not otherwise entertain. The one who expounds a text teases or jolts us into the possibility that it opens for us a horizon that we would otherwise be too cooped up to see. The words of Luther about the words of Jesus in the Gospel may lead us to consider seriously trusting where we have not trusted, praying where we might have lost interest in prayer, and feeling blessed where we had once felt abandoned.

Thus Jesus and Luther have their own horizons, and we fuse these with our own. In order to discern what is on their horizons, we have to be a bit patient. Their worlds were closer to nature than our citified worlds. They used themes from agriculture, and we would use some from industry. They found it easy, very easy, to speak about the devil as a person and force around us and in us. We find that more difficult—strangely, in this century of the concentration camp, gross torture, and inhuman ideology. Our world and their worlds may not exactly fit. That is the point. We do not learn when we deal with what already fits. We entertain new possibilities when we are shocked into them. Do not expect Luther to speak as a liberated feminist, a modern republican, a smooth manager. Do expect his horizon to be one in which modern people who would be liberated, politic, and successful are addressed. They will find their way into Luther's world. Then they must make their way beyond it —into their own. Along that path, the beckoning comes from Jesus who walks ahead of us, demanding, inviting trust in the Trustworthy One. To that One we are invited to say, "I am sure that you will not betray my hope, that you will respond to it, that you will fulfill it." Or, as Jesus put it in Matthew 6:9, "Pray, then, like this: . . ."

1. "DO NOT BE ANXIOUS"

On Matthew 6:25–7:11

Therefore I tell you, do not be concerned about your life, what you shall eat or what you shall drink, nor about your body, what you shall put on. Is not life more than food, and the body more than clothing? (6:25)

Listen . . . to what serving *Mammon* [the god of possession] means. It means being concerned about our life and our body, about what we should eat and drink and put on. It means thinking only about this life, about how to get rich here and how to accumulate and increase our money and property, as though we were going to stay here forever. The sinful worship of Mammon does not consist in eating and drinking and wearing clothes, nor in looking for a way to make a living and working at it; for the needs of this life and of the body make food and clothing a requirement. But the sin consists in being concerned about it and making it the reliance and confidence of your heart. Concern does not stick to clothing or to food, but directly to the heart, which cannot let a thing go and has to hang on to it. As the saying goes, "Property makes a person bold." Thus "being concerned" means clinging to it with your heart. I am not concerned about anything that my heart does not think about, but I must have a heart for anything about which I am concerned.

You must not tighten this text too much, however, as if it prohibited any kind of concern at all. Every office and station involves taking on certain concerns, especially being in charge of other people. As St. Paul says about spiritual offices in Christendom (Rom. 12:8): "He who rules, let him be careful." In this sense the head of a household has to be concerned about whether his children are being brought up properly; . . . if he neglects this, he does wrong. . . .

Christ is not talking here about this sort of concern. This is an official concern, which must be sharply distinguished from greed. It is not concerned for its own sake but for the neighbor's sake; it does not seek its own interests (1 Cor. 13:5), but even neglects them and forgets them in order to serve somebody else. Therefore it may be called a concern of love, something divine and Christian, not a concern devoted to its own advantage or to Mammon, militating against faith and love, and even interfering with the official concern. The man whose money is dear to him and who is on the lookout for his own advantage will not have much regard for his neighbor or for the office that involves his neighbor. . . .

Christ has forbidden this greedy concern and worship of Mammon as an idolatry that makes men enemies of God. Now He goes on with many statements, examples, and illustrations, intended to make greed so repulsive to us and to give it such an odious appearance that we will feel like spitting on it. First of all He says: "Is not life more than food? That is, you can and you must entrust your life, your body, and your soul to God. It does not lie within your power to preserve this for a single hour. What fools you are, then, if you do not entrust the needs of your body to Him, too, for Him to provide you with food and drink! It would be the greatest foolishness imaginable to be scrupulously concerned about getting food and drink but to be unconcerned about getting body and life or preserving them for an hour. That would be like being concerned about the beautiful decoration of your house but not knowing who was going to live there, or being concerned in the kitchen about the preparation of a big, expensive meal but not having anybody to eat it." That is how we behave in our greed: we are concerned about the little things, and we never think of the big things. Such concern is really unnecessary and superfluous, in fact, foolish. Even though we were to be deeply concerned about our body and its life, this would not accomplish a thing, since it does not lie within our power even for a moment, any more than grain growing in a field where we did not do the planting, or silver in a mine where we did not put it. . . .

. . . Yet we go along in our blindness, although it is obvious that we should not be concerned about our body and life. Even if we were concerned, that in itself would have to make us become Christians and think: "You see, not even for a moment do I have my life in my own hands. Now, since I have to entrust my body and life to God, why should I have any doubts and concerns about my belly and about how it is to be fed for a day or two?" It is like having a rich father who would be willing to give me a thousand guldens, and then not trusting him to give me a groschen when I need it.

Look at the birds of the air: they neither sow nor reap nor gather into barns, and yet your heavenly Father feeds them. Are you not of more value than they? And which of you by being anxious can add one cubit to his stature? (6:26–27)

You see, He is making the birds our schoolmasters and teachers. It is a great and abiding disgrace to us that in the Gospel a helpless sparrow should become a theologian and a preacher to the wisest of men, and daily should emphasize this to our eyes and ears, as if he were saying to us: "Look, you miserable man! You have house and home, money and property. Every year you have a field full of grain and other plants of all sorts, more than you ever need. Yet you cannot find peace, and you are always worried about starving. If you do not know that you have supplies and cannot see them before your very eyes, you cannot trust God to give you food for one day. Though we are innumerable, none of us spends his living days worrying. Still God feeds us every day." In other words, we have as many teachers and preachers as there are little birds in the air. Their living example is an embarrassment to us. Whenever we hear a bird singing toward heaven and proclaiming God's praises and our disgrace, we should feel ashamed and not even dare to lift up our eyes. But we are as hard as stone, and we pay no attention even though we hear the great multitude preaching and singing every day.

Look at what else the dear little birds do. Their life is completely unconcerned, and they wait for their food solely from the hands of God. Sometimes people cage them up to hear them sing. Then they get food in abundance, and they ought to think: "Now I have plenty. I do not have to be concerned about where my food is coming from. Now I have a rich master, and my barns are full." But they do not do this. When they are free in the air, they are happier and fatter. Their singing of Lauds and of Matins to their Lord early in the morning before they eat is more excellent and more pleasant. Yet none of them knows of a single grain laid away in store. They sing a lovely, long Benedicite and leave their cares to our Lord God, even when they have young that have to be fed. Whenever you listen to a nightingale, therefore, you are listening to an excellent preacher. He exhorts you with this Gospel, not with mere simple words but with a living deed and an example. He sings all night and practically screams his lungs out. He is happier in the woods than cooped up in a cage, where he has to be taken care of constantly and where he rarely gets along very well or even stays alive. It is as if he were saying: "I prefer to be in the Lord's kitchen. He has made heaven and earth, and He Himself is the cook and the host. Every day He feeds and nourishes innumerable little birds out of His hand. For He does not have merely a bag full of grain, but heaven and earth."

Now Christ says: "Every day you see before your very eyes how the heavenly Father feeds the little birds in the field, without any concern on their part. Can you not trust Him to feed you as well, since He is your Father and calls you His children? Shall He not be concerned about you, whom He has made

His children and to whom He gives His Word and all creatures, more than about the little birds, which are not His children but your servants? And yet He thinks enough of them to feed them every day, as if they were the only thing He is concerned about. And He enjoys it when they fly around and sing without a care in the world, as if they were saying: 'I sing and frolic, and yet I do not know of a single grain that I am to eat. My bread is not baked yet, and my grain is not planted yet. But I have a rich Master who takes care of me while I am singing or sleeping. He can give me more than all my worries and the worries of all people could ever accomplish.' " Now, since the birds have learned so well the art of trusting Him and of casting their cares from themselves upon God, we who are His children should do so even more. Thus this is an excellent illustration that puts us all to shame. We, who are rational people and who have the Scriptures in addition, do not have enough wisdom to imitate the birds. When we listen to the little birds singing every day, we are listening to our own embarrassment before God and the people. But after his fall from the word and the commandment of God, man became crazy and foolish; and there is no creature alive which is not wiser than he. A little finch, which can neither speak nor read, is his theologian and master in the Scriptures, even though he has the whole Bible and his reason to help him. . . .

And why are you anxious about clothing? Consider the lilies of the field, how they grow; they neither toil nor spin; yet I tell you, even Solomon in all his glory was not arrayed like one of these. But if God so clothes the grass of the field, which today is alive and tomorrow is thrown into the oven, will He not much more clothe you, O men of little faith? (6:28–30)

Here you have another example and analogy; according to it, the little flowers in the field, which cattle trample and eat, are to become our theologians and masters and to embarrass us still further. Just look at them grow, all adorned with lovely colors! Yet not one of them is anxious or worried about how it should grow or what color it should have, but it leaves these anxieties to God. And without any care or effort on its part God dresses it up in such lovely and beautiful colors that, as Christ says, King Solomon in all his glory was not so beautiful as one of these—indeed, no empress with all her ladies-in-waiting, with all her gold, pearls, and jewels. No king He could name was so rich or so glorious or so beautifully adorned as was Solomon. But with all his magnificent pomp and splendor, the king is nothing when compared with a rose or a pink or a violet in the field. In this way our Lord God can adorn anyone whom He chooses to adorn. That is really an adornment, a color that no man can make or match, an adornment that no one could or would surpass. Though they were to be covered with pure gold and satin, they would still say: "I prefer the adornment of my Master up there in heaven, who adorns the little birds, to that of all the tailors and embroiderers on earth."

Now, since He dresses and adorns so many flowers with such a variety of colors, and each has its own coat, more splendid than all the adornment in the world, why is it that we cannot have faith that He will dress us as well? What are the flowers and the grass in the field when compared with us? And what were they created for except to stand there for a day or two, to let themselves be looked at, and then to wither and turn into hay? Or as Christ says, they are "thrown into the oven" to be burned and to heat the oven. Yet our Lord God regards these tiny and transient things so highly that He lavishes His gifts upon them and adorns them more beautifully than any earthly king or other human being. Yet they do not need this adornment; indeed, it is wasted upon them, since, with the flower, it soon perishes. But we are His highest creatures, for whose sakes He made all things and to whom He gives everything. We matter so much to Him that this life is not to be the end of us, but after this life He intends to give us eternal life. Now, should we not trust Him to clothe us as He clothes the flowers of the field with so many colors and the birds of the air with their lovely feathers? He is speaking satirically, in order to describe how abominable our unbelief is and to make it look as ridiculous as possible. . . . They sing and preach to us and smile at us so lovingly, just to have us believe. And yet we go right on letting them preach and sing, while we remain as greedy and selfish as ever. But to our eternal shame and disgrace each individual flower is a witness against us to condemn our unbelief before God and all the creatures until the Last Day. . . .

Therefore do not be anxious, saying, "What shall we eat?" or, "What shall we drink?" or, "What shall we wear?" For the Gentiles seek all these things; and your heavenly Father knows that you need them all. (6: 31–32)

Every day you see these illustrations before your very eyes, how God nourishes and feeds everything that lives and grows from the earth, clothes and adorns it so beautifully. Now let these illustrations persuade you to lay aside your anxiety and your unbelief and to remember that you are Christians and not heathen. Such anxiety and greed are appropriate to heathen, who do not know God or care about Him. It is really idolatry, as St. Paul says (Eph. 5:5; Col. 3:5). . . .

"Since you are Christians," He says, "you dare not doubt that your Father is well aware of your need for all this, of the fact that you have a belly that needs food and drink and a body that needs clothing. If He did not know it, you would have reason to be concerned and anxious about how to provide for yourselves. But since He does know it, He will not forsake you. He is faithful and willing to take special care of you Christians, because, as has been said, He cares for the birds of the air as well. So forget your anxieties, since you cannot accomplish anything by them. It does not depend upon your anxiety but upon His knowledge and concern." If nothing grew in the field unless we were anxious about it, we would all have died in our cradles; and during the night, while we are lying asleep, nothing could grow. Indeed, even by worrying ourselves to death we could not make a single blade of grass grow in the field. We really ought to see and understand that God gives every-thing without any anxiety on our part, and yet we are such godless people that we refuse to give up our anxiety and our greed. Though it is up to Him to be concerned, as a father is concerned for his children, we refuse to leave it to Him.

But seek first the kingdom of God and His righteous-
ness, and all these things shall be yours as well. (6:33)

. . . It is important for the heart to realize what
the kingdom of God is and what it grants. If we
could be persuaded to give this some thought and
if in our hearts we were to measure and weigh how
much greater and more precious a treasure this is
than Mammon or the kingdom of the world, that is,
than everything on earth, then we would spit at
Mammon. If you had the wealth and the might of
the King of France and of the Turkish Emperor,
what more would you have than a beggar at the
door has with his crumbs? All that is really necessary is something to fill the belly every day. More
than this no one can do, even if he has all the goods
and all the glory in the world. The poorest beggar
has as much of this as the mightiest emperor; and
he may even get more enjoyment and benefit out of
his crumbs than the emperor does out of a magnificent, royal repast. That is all there is to it, and no
one gets any more out of it. It lasts only a brief and
tiny while, and then we have to surrender it all. We
cannot use it to extend our physical existence by a
single hour when our hour comes. . . .

By these words, therefore, Christ would like to
wake us up and say: "If you want to have the right
sort of anxiety and concern about always having

plenty, then seek for the treasure called 'the kingdom of God.' Do not be anxious about the temporal and perishable treasure which moth and rust consume. . . . You have a much different treasure in heaven, which I am pointing out to you. If you are anxious about that and seek it and if you keep in mind what you have in it, you will soon forget about the other one. This is the kind of treasure that will sustain you forever, and it cannot perish or be taken away. Because the treasure you cling to is an enduring one, you will endure, too, even though you may not have a single [dollar] from the world."

What the kingdom of God is has often been stated. To put it most briefly, it does not mean outward things like eating and drinking (Rom. 14: 17) nor other works that we can do. Rather, it means believing in Jesus Christ. In this kingdom He is the Head and the only King, in whom and through whom we have everything; whoever abides in it cannot be harmed by any sin, death, or misfortune, but has eternal life, joy, and salvation. Here he begins in this faith, but on the Last Day all will be revealed, and he will be eternally perfected in it.

Now, what does it mean to "seek" this kingdom? What is the method of reaching it, and what way or path leads to it? Here one points in one direction, another in another direction. . . . For there are many ways, but they are all departures from that one way of believing in Christ and practicing and applying the Gospel, to which faith clings. This involves growing and being strengthened at heart through preaching, listening, reading, singing, meditating, and every other possible way. And it involves blossoming out in fruits, to advance it and to lead many other people to it. . . . If you want to know [the Kingdom] and find it, you must not seek for it on the basis of your own ideas. You must hear His Word, as the foundation and cornerstone, and see where He directs you and how He interprets it. Now, this is His Word about His kingdom (Mark 16:16): "He who believes and is baptized will be saved." The Word was not spun out of our own heads, nor did it grow out of any human heart. It fell from heaven and was manifested by the mouth of God, to give us certainty and to keep us from missing the right path. Now when both the preachers and the hearers proceed as they should in the diligent use of Word and Sacrament, when they consistently apply this in their lives to make it known among the people, and when they bring in the young people and teach them, then they are really seeking and promoting the kingdom of God and taking it seriously.

Now, what does He mean by adding "and His righteousness"? This kingdom has a righteousness of its own, but a righteousness different from that in the world, since it is a different kingdom. Thus it refers to the righteousness that comes from a faith that is busy and active in good works. It means that I take the Gospel seriously, that I listen to it or use it diligently, and that then I actually live in accordance with it instead of being an idle fellow or a hypocrite, who lets it come in through one ear and out through the other. The Kingdom proves its presence in deed and in power, as St. Paul says (1 Cor. 4:20): "The kingdom of God does not consist in talk but in power." That is what we call the Gospel with its fruits—doing good works, fulfilling your station or office diligently and faithfully, and undergoing all sorts of suffering for the Gospel. He uses "righteousness" here in a general sense for the whole life of a Christian in relation to God and man, including both the tree and its fruit, not in the sense that it is completely perfect. It is continually progressing, as He shows here by telling His disciples to keep on seeking it, since they have not yet obtained it (Phil. 3:12) or learned it or lived it perfectly. For our condition in the kingdom of Christ is half sin and half holiness. What there is in us that belongs to faith and to Christ is completely pure and perfect, since it is not our own but Christ's, who is ours through faith and who lives and works in us. But what is still our own is completely sinful. Yet under Christ and in Him it is concealed and blotted out through the forgiveness of sins; and daily it is put to death through the same grace of the Spirit, until we have died to this life altogether. . . .

. . . To [His] admonition He now adds a promise and a consolation, to keep us from thinking that since we have to suffer so much from a world that denies and begrudges us everything and since every hour we are expecting to have it all taken away from us, He wants to give us nothing at all on earth and to let us starve. We should know that here, too, we shall have what we require for the necessities of this life. That is why He says: "If you just seek the kingdom of God first, then all these things shall be yours as well." That is, you shall receive food and drink and clothing as a bonus, without any anxiety of your own. In fact, it will come by the very fact that you are not anxious about such things and that you risk everything for the sake of the kingdom of God, and in such a way that you will not know where it came from, as our experience teaches us every day. . . .

Therefore do not be anxious about tomorrow, for tomorrow will be anxious for itself. Let the day's own trouble be sufficient for the day. (6:34)

"Let this be your concern," He says, "how to retain the kingdom of God. And get rid of the other concerns so completely that you are not even concerned about tomorrow. When tomorrow comes, it will bring its own concerns along." As we say, "Do not cross your bridges until you come to them." Our concern accomplishes nothing anyway, even though we are concerned for only one day at a time. Experience shows that two or three days often pass by faster than today. If God is kindly disposed to a man and gives him success, he can often accomplish more in one hour without care and anxiety than another man in four whole days with great care and anxiety. Whereas the one has dragged on with his anxiety and made it tedious for himself, the other has disposed of it in an hour. Thus no one can accomplish anything except when the hour comes that God gives as a free gift without our anxiety. It is vain for you to try to anticipate and with your concern to work out what you think are great schemes.

Our Lord God knows the art of secretly shortening and lengthening times and hours for us, to make one hour become two weeks for someone, and vice versa. Thus with long labor and sorrow one person accomplishes no more than another person with short and easy work. This is evident every day. There are many people who work steadily and hard but barely make ends meet, while there are others who have arranged and ordered their affairs so well that without any particular effort everything goes along smoothly, and they prosper. God works it all this way to keep us from supposing that our anxiety necessarily brings His blessing. But we refuse to wait for God to add these good things to us. Instead we insist on finding them for ourselves before God gives them. . . .

Now, since you see that it is pointless and that your anxiety is useless, why not give it up and think instead about how to get the kingdom of God? He wants to be generous to you, but not on account of your being concerned or even on account of your working. It is not such concern that gains and accomplishes anything, but rather the concern that is part of your office. The kingdom of God requires you to do what you are commanded to do, to preach and to promote the Word of God, to serve your neighbor according to your calling, and to take whatever God gives you. The best possessions are not the ones that come from our planning, but the ones that come by chance and from His generosity. The things that we have acquired or planned to keep by being anxious will probably be the first to collapse and be ruined. . . . It is a great gift of grace that God does not make it our concern how the grain is growing in the field, but gives it to us while we are lying asleep. Otherwise we would ruin it with our anxiety, and we would get nothing.

Therefore He says now: "Why be concerned about more than the present day and take on the troubles of two days? Be content with the trouble that the present day lays upon you. Tomorrow will bring you another one." He calls it a "trouble" or a plague laid upon us that we have to make a living in the sweat of our face (Gen. 3:19) and endure all sorts of other accidents, worries, misfortunes, and dangers every day. Daily in this life we must see and expect such trouble, when something is stolen from you or you suffer some other damage or when you get sick or when your servants do. Suffer such sorrow, anguish, and trouble, and receive it with joy. Be content with that, for it is enough for you to bear. Forget about your anxiety, which only increases and aggravates the trouble. From these examples you can see that God never used anyone's anxiety to make him rich; in fact, many people have the deepest kind of anxiety, and still they have nothing. What He does is this: when He sees someone fulfilling his office diligently and faithfully, being concerned to do so in a God-pleasing way, and leaving the concern over its success to God, He is generous in His gifts to such a person. It is written (Prov. 10:4): "The hand of the diligent makes rich."

. . . He commands you to get an honest grip on your work, and then He will be present with His blessing and give you plenty. . . .

Ask, and it will be given you; seek, and you will find; knock, and it will be opened to you. For every one who asks, receives, and he who seeks, finds, and to him who knocks it will be opened. Or what man of you, if his son asks him for a loaf, will give him a stone? Or if he asks for a fish, will give him a serpent? If you, then, who are evil, know how to give good gifts to your children, how much more will your Father who is in heaven give good things to those who ask Him? (7: 7–11)

. . . Christ, the Lord . . . adds an admonition to prayer. By this He intends to teach [his disciples] that, second only to the office of preaching, prayer is the chief work of a Christian. . . . He also wants to indicate that because of all the temptations and hindrances we face, nothing is more necessary in Christendom than continual and unceasing prayer that God would give His grace and His Spirit to make the doctrine powerful and efficacious among us and among others. That is why, in the words [of] the prophet Zechariah (Zech. 12:10), God promised that He would pour out upon the Christians a Spirit of grace and of supplication. In these two items He summarizes all Christian existence.

Now, what He intends to say is this: "I have given you instructions about how you ought to live and what you ought to watch out for. In addition, it is necessary that you ask and that you have the confidence to go right on seeking and knocking without becoming lazy or lax in it. You will have need of asking, seeking, and knocking." Though doctrine and life may both have begun all right, we shall have to suffer from all sorts of transgressions and offenses that hinder us daily and keep us from progressing. We battle against these continually with all our might, but the strongest shield we have is prayer. If we do not use that, it is impossible for us to hold our own and to go on being Christians. We can plainly see now not only the sort of obstacles that oppose the Gospel every day, but also our own neglect of prayer and our attitude, as though this warning and admonition did not refer to us and we did not need prayer any more. . . . All this is not a good sign, and it makes me afraid that some great misfortune which we could have prevented will overtake us.

Therefore every Christian should pay attention to this admonition. It is, in the first place, a commandment, as much as the previous statement, "Judge not," is a commandment. He should know that he is obliged to practice this Christian work. He should not be like that peasant who said: "I give grain to my minister, and he prays for me"; or like the people who think: "What is the use of my pray-ing? If I do not pray, others do." We must not suppose that it is no concern of ours or that it is left up to our free choice. . . . In the second place, you have here the comforting promise and rich assurance that He attaches to prayer, to make it evident that He cares about it and to teach us to think about prayer as something dear and precious before God, because His admonition is so serious and His invitation so friendly, and He promises that we shall not ask in vain. Even if we had no other reason or attraction than this rich and friendly word, it should be enough to prompt us to pray. I shall not even talk about how dear His exhortation is or how sublime His command or how desperate our need.

Our own desperate need should be enough to make us pray. But in addition, as though that were not enough, He seeks to draw us to it by means of the beautiful analogy of every father's relation to his son. Though the son may be a good-for-nothing scamp, still he will not give him a serpent when he asks him for a fish. From that he draws these consoling words: "If you can do this, though you do not have a good nature or a single good trait in comparison with God, will not God, your heavenly Father, whose nature is completely good, give you good things if you ask Him for them?" This is the most sublime attraction by which anyone can be persuaded to pray, if we just looked at these words and took them to heart.

We have already spoken of the need that prompts Him to give this admonition and should prompt us to ask. Once you have the Word of God right and have made a good start in both doctrine and life, then inevitably temptation and opposition arise, not one kind but thousands of kinds. In the first place, there is our own flesh. . . . It quickly becomes bored, inattentive, and indifferent to the Word of God and the good life. Thus we always have less of wisdom and of the Word of God, of faith and love and patience, than we should. This is the first enemy hanging around our neck so heavily every day that he keeps dragging us that way. Next comes the second enemy, the world. It begrudges us the dear Word and faith and refuses to put up with anything in us, no matter how weak we may be. It goes ahead and condemns us, it tries to take away what we have, and it gives us no peace. . . .

But getting ourselves to the point of praying causes us distress and anguish, and this requires the greatest skill. With our own concerns and thoughts we torture ourselves and stew over trying to pull this off our neck and to get rid of it. There is an evil and clever devil riding me and other people and frequently playing these tricks on me in my temptation or anxiety, whether it has to do with spiritual or with secular affairs. He immediately butts in and makes you start stewing over it. In this way he snatches us from our prayer and makes us so dizzy that we do not even think of praying. By the time you begin praying you have already tortured yourself half to death. He is well aware of what prayer achieves and can do. That is why he creates so many obstacles and disturbances, to keep you from getting around to it at all. Hence we ought to learn to take these words to heart. We should develop the habit, whenever we see anguish or need, to fall on our knees immediately and to spread the need before God, on the basis of this admonition and promise. Then we would find help and would not have to torture ourselves with our own ideas about looking for help. This is a very precious medicine, one that certainly helps and never fails, if you will only use it. . . .

Why does Christ use so many words? He lists three items: "Ask, and it will be given you; seek, and you will find; knock, and it will be opened to you." One would have been enough. It is evident . . . that by this He intends to admonish us even more strongly to pray. He knows that we are timid and shy, that we feel unworthy and unfit to present our needs to God. We feel the needs, but we cannot express them. We think that God is so great and we are so tiny that we do not dare to pray. . . . That is why Christ wants to lure us away from such timid thoughts, to remove our doubts, and to have us go ahead confidently and boldly. Though I am unworthy, I am still His creature; and since He has made me worthy of being His creature, I am also worthy of receiving what He has promised and so generously offered to me. In other words, if I am unworthy, He and His promise are not unworthy. You can venture on this vigorously and trustfully, you can put it in His lap joyfully and confidently. But above all, be sure that you really believe in Christ and that you have a proper occupation, one that pleases God, so that you are not like the world, which does not care about its occupation but only about the vices and the villainy that it goes right on planning day and night. . . .

. . . For you have His Word, and He will have to say: "All right, then, you may have what you want." St. James speaks of this in his Epistle when he says (James 5:16): "The prayer of a righteous man has great power in its effects" if it is serious and persistent; and in support of this he cites the example from the Scriptures of the prophet Elijah (James 5:16, 17). By urging you not only to ask but also to knock, God intends to test you to see whether you can hold on tight, and to teach you that your prayer is not displeasing to Him or unheard, simply because His answer is delayed and you are permitted to go on seeking and knocking.

2. "WHEN YOU PRAY"

On Matthew 6:5–13

And when you pray, you must not be like the hypocrites; for they love to stand and pray in the synagogs and at the street corners, that they may be seen by men. Truly, I say to you, they have their reward. But when you pray, go into your room and shut the door and pray to your Father who is in secret; and your Father who sees in secret will reward you. (6:5–6)

Here the emphasis is on the fact that [petition] must be a genuine prayer and not a piece of hypocrisy. . . . Therefore, in instructing them how to pray correctly, Christ begins by showing them how they should go about it: they are not supposed to stand and pray publicly on the streets, but they should pray at home, in their own room, alone, in secret. This means that, above all, they should rid themselves of the false motive of praying for the sake of the appearance or reputation or anything of that sort. It does not mean that prayer on the street or in public is prohibited; for a Christian is not bound to any particular place and may pray anywhere, whether he is on the street or in the field or in church. All it means is that this must not be done out of regard for other people, as a means of getting glory or profit. In the same way He does not forbid the blowing of a trumpet or the ringing of a bell at almsgiving for its own sake, but He denounces the addition of a false motivation when He says: "in order to be seen by men."

Nor is it a necessary part of this commandment that you have to go into a room and lock yourself in. Still, it is a good idea for a person to be alone when he intends to pray, so that he can pour out his prayer to God in a free and uninhibited manner, using words and gestures that he could not use if he were in human company. Although it is true that prayer can take place in the heart without any words or gestures, yet such things help in stirring up and enkindling the spirit even more; but in addition, the praying should continue in the heart almost without interruption. As we have said, a Christian always has the Spirit of supplication with him, and his heart is continually sending forth sighs and petitions to God, regardless of whether he happens to be eating or drinking or working. For his entire life is devoted to spreading the name of God, His glory, and His kingdom, so that whatever else he may do has to be subordinated to this.

Nevertheless, I say, outward prayer must also go on, both individual prayer and corporate prayer. In the morning and in the evening, at table and whenever he has time, every individual should speak a benediction or the Our Father or the Creed or a psalm. And in assemblies the Word of God should be employed and thanks and petitions voiced to God for our general needs. This must necessarily be done in public, with a special time and place set aside for such assemblies. Such prayer is a precious thing and a powerful defense against the devil and his assaults. For in it, all Christendom combines its forces with one accord; and the harder it prays, the more effective it is and the sooner it is heard. . . . Thus it is certain that whatever still stands and endures, whether it is in the spiritual or in the secular realm, is being preserved through prayer.

[I shall only summarize . . . briefly here] the component parts and the characteristics which every real prayer has to possess. . . . They are as follows: first, the urging of God's commandment, who has strictly required us to pray; second, His promise, in which He declares that He will hear us; third, an examination of our own need and misery, which burden lies so heavily on our shoulders that we have to carry it to God immediately and pour it out before Him, in accordance with His order and commandment; fourth, true faith, based on this word and promise of God, praying with the certainty and confidence that He will hear and help us—and all these things in the name of Christ, through whom our prayer is acceptable to the Father and for whose sake He gives us every grace and every good.

Christ indicates this by His use of one word when He says: "Pray to your Father who is in secret"; and later on He makes it even more explicit when He says: "Our Father who art in heaven." For this is the same as teaching that our prayer should be addressed to God as our gracious and friendly father, not as a tyrant or an angry judge. Now, no one can do this unless he has a word of God which says that He wants to have us call Him "Father" and that as a father He has promised to hear us and help us. To do this, one must also have such a faith in his heart and a happy courage to call God his Father, praying on the basis of a hearty confidence, relying upon the certainty that the prayer will be heard, and then waiting for help.

Learn, therefore, that there can be no real prayer without this faith. But do you feel weak and fearful? Your flesh and blood is always putting obstacles in the way of faith, as if you were not worthy enough or ready enough or earnest enough to pray. Or do you doubt that God has heard you, since you are a sinner? Then hold on to the Word and say: "Though I am sinful and unworthy, still I have the commandment of God, telling me to pray, and His promise that He will graciously hear me, not on account of my worthiness, but on account of the Lord Christ." In this way you can chase away the thoughts and the doubts, and you can cheerfully kneel down to pray. You need not consider whether you are worthy or unworthy; all you need to consider is your need and His Word, on which He tells you to build. This is especially so because He has set before you the manner of praying and put into your mouth the words you are to use when you pray, as follows here. Thus you may joyfully send up these prayers through Him and put them into His bosom, so that through His own merit He may bring them before the Father.

And in praying do not heap up empty phrases as the Gentiles do; for they think that they will be heard for their many words. Do not be like them, for your Father knows what you need before you ask Him. Pray, then, like this:

> *Our Father who art in heaven,*
> *Hallowed be Thy name.*
> *Thy kingdom come.*
> *Thy will be done,*
>   *On earth as it is in heaven.*
> *Give us this day our daily bread;*

And forgive us our debts,
    As we also have forgiven our debtors;
And lead us not into temptation,
    But deliver us from evil.
For Thine is the kingdom and the power and the
    glory, forever. Amen. (6:7–13)

. . . The Christian's prayer is easy, and it does not cause hard work. For it proceeds in faith on the basis of the promise of God, and it presents its need from the heart. Faith quickly gets through telling what it wants; indeed, it does so with a sigh that the heart utters and that words can neither attain nor express. As Paul says (Rom. 8:26), "the Spirit prays." And because He knows that God is listening to Him, He has no need of such everlasting twaddle. That is how the saints prayed in the Scriptures, like Elijah, Elisha, David, and others—with brief but strong and powerful words. This is evident in the Psalter, where there is hardly a single psalm that has a prayer more than five or six verses long. Therefore the ancient fathers have said correctly that many long prayers are not the way. They recommend short, fervent prayers, where one sighs toward heaven with a word or two, as is often quite possible in the midst of reading, writing, or doing some other task.

But the others, who make it nothing but a work

of drudgery, can never pray with gladness or with devotion. They are glad when they are finally through with their babbling. And so it must be. Where there is no faith and no feeling of need in a petition, there the heart cannot be involved either. But where the heart is not involved and the body has to do all the work, there it becomes difficult drudgery. This is evident even in physical work. How difficult and dreary it is for the person who is doing something unwillingly! But on the other hand, if the heart is cheerful and willing, then it does not even notice the work. So it is here, too: the man who is serious in his intentions and takes pleasure in prayer neither knows nor feels any toil and trouble; he simply looks at his need, and he has finished singing or praying the words before he has a chance to turn around. In other words, prayers ought to be brief, frequent, and intense. For God does not ask how much and how long you have prayed, but how good the prayer is and whether it proceeds from the heart.

Therefore Christ says now: "Your heavenly Father knows what you need before you ask for it." It is as if He would say: "What are you up to? Do you suppose that you will talk Him down with your long babbling and make Him give you what you need? There is no need for you to persuade Him with your words or to give Him detailed instructions; for He knows beforehand what you need, even better than you do yourself." If you came before a prince or a judge who knew your case better than you could describe it to him and tried to give him a long-winded account of it, he would have a perfect right to laugh at you or, more likely, to become displeased with you. Indeed, as St. Paul says (Rom. 8:26), "We do not know how we are to pray." Therefore when He hears us, whatever He gives us is something in excess of our understanding or our hopes. Sometimes He lets us go on asking for something which He does not give right away, or perhaps does not give at all, knowing very well what is necessary and useful for us and what is not. We ourselves do not see this, but finally we have to admit that it would not have been good for us if He had done His giving on the basis of our petition. Therefore we must not go into a long harangue to give Him instructions or prescriptions about what He should do for us and how He should do it. He intends to give in such a way that His name might be hallowed, His kingdom extended, and His will advanced.

But you may say: "Since He knows and sees all our needs better than we do ourselves, why does He let us bring our petitions and present our need, instead of giving it to us without our petitioning? After all, He freely gives the whole world so much good every day, like the sun, the rain, crops and money, body and life, for which no one asks Him or thanks Him. He knows that no one can get along for a single day without light, food, and drink. Then why does He tell us to ask for these things?"

The reason He commands it is, of course, not in order to have us make our prayers an instruction to Him as to what He ought to give us, but in order to have us acknowledge and confess that He is already bestowing many blessings upon us and that He can and will give us still more. By our praying, therefore, we are instructing ourselves more than we are Him. It makes me turn around so that I do not proceed as do the ungodly, neither acknowledging this nor thanking Him for it. When my heart is turned to Him and awakened this way, then I praise Him, thank Him, take refuge with Him in my need, and expect help from Him. As a consequence of all this, I learn more and more to acknowledge what kind of God He is. Because I seek and knock at His door (Matt. 7:7), He takes pleasure in giving me ever more generous gifts. You see, that is how a genuine petitioner proceeds. He is not like those other useless babblers, who prattle a great deal but who never recognize all this. He knows that what he has is a gift of God, and from his heart he says: "Lord, I know that of myself I can neither produce nor preserve a piece of my daily bread; nor can I defend myself against any kind of need or misfortune. Therefore I shall look to Thee for it and request it from Thee, since Thou dost command me this way and dost promise to give it to me, Thou who dost anticipate my every thought and sympathize with my every need."

You see, a prayer that acknowledges this truly pleases God. It is the truest, highest, and most precious worship which we can render to Him; for it gives Him the glory that is due Him. . . . A Christian heart is one that learns from the Word of God that everything we have is from God and nothing is from ourselves. Such a heart accepts all this in faith and practices it, learning to look to Him for everything and to expect it from Him. In this way praying teaches us to recognize who we are and who God is, and to learn what we need and where we are to look for it and find it. The result of this is an excellent, perfect, and sensible man, one who can maintain the right relationship to all things.

Having denounced and rejected . . . false and useless prayers, Christ now proceeds to introduce an excellent and brief formula. It shows how we are to pray and what we are to pray for. It includes all sorts of needs which ought to impel us to pray and of which we can daily remind ourselves with these short words. There is no excuse for anyone now, as though he did not know how or what to pray.

Hence it is a very good practice . . . to pray the entire Lord's Prayer every day, morning and evening and at table, and otherwise, too, as a way of presenting all sorts of general needs to God. . . .

As has often been said . . . this is certainly the very best prayer that ever came to earth or that anyone could ever have thought up. Because God the Father composed it through His Son and placed it into His mouth, there is no need for us to doubt that it pleases Him immensely. At the very beginning He warns us to remember both his command and His promise, in the word "Our Father." He it is who demands this glory from us, that we should put our petitions to Him, as a child does to its father. He also wants us to have the confidence that He will gladly give us what we need. Also included is the reminder that we should glory in being His children through Christ. And so we come, on the basis of His command and His promise, and in the name of Christ, the Lord; and we present ourselves before Him with all confidence.

Now the first, second, and third petitions deal with the highest benefits that we receive from Him. In the first place, because He is our Father, He should receive from us the glory that is due Him, and His name should be held in high esteem throughout the world. By this petition I pile up on one heap every kind of false belief and worship, all of hell, and all sin and blasphemy. And I ask Him to put a stop to . . . all . . . who . . . desecrate and profane His name or seek their own glory under the pretext of His name. This is indeed only a brief phrase, but its meaning extends as far as the world and opposes all false doctrine and life.

In the second place, once we have His Word, true doctrine, and true worship, we also pray that His kingdom may be in us and remain in us; that is, that He may govern us in this doctrine and life, that He may protect and preserve us against all the power of the devil and his kingdom, and that He may shatter all the kingdoms that rage against His kingdom, so that it alone may remain. And in the third place, we pray that neither our will nor any other man's will, but His will alone may be done, and that what He plans and counsels may succeed and overcome all the schemes and undertakings of the world, as well as anything else that may set itself against His plans and counsels, even though the whole world were to mass itself and rally all its strength to defend its cause against Him. These are the three most important elements.

In the other four petitions we meet the needs that apply to our own daily life and to this poor, weak, and temporal existence. Therefore our first petition here is that He may give us our daily bread—that is, everything necessary for the preservation of this life, like food, a healthy body, good weather, house, home, wife, children, good government, and peace —and that He may preserve us from all sorts of calamities, sickness, pestilence, hard times, war, revolution, and the like. Our next petition is this: that He may forgive us our debts and not look upon the shameful and thankless way we misuse the benefits with which He daily provides us in such abundance; that this may not prompt Him to deny us these benefits or to withdraw them or to punish us with the disfavor we deserve; but that He may graciously pardon us, although we who are called "Christians" and "children of God" do not live as we should. The third of these petitions is brought on by the fact that we are living on earth, amid all sorts of temptation and trouble, with attacks from every side. Thus the source of the hindrance and the temptation we experience is not only external, from the world and the devil, but also internal, from our own flesh. Amid so much danger and temptation, we cannot live the way we should; nor would we be able to stand it for a single day. We ask Him, therefore, to sustain us in the midst of this danger and need so that it does not overcome and destroy us. And our final petition is that He would ultimately deliver us completely from all evil, and when the time comes for us to pass out of this life, that He would bestow upon us a gracious and blessed hour of death. In this brief compass we have laid all our physical and spiritual needs into

His lap, and each individual word has summarized an entire world of meaning.

But in the text there is a small addition with which He concludes the prayer, a sort of thanksgiving and common confession, namely this: "For Thine is the kingdom and the power and the glory, forever." These are really the titles and names that are appropriate to God alone, for these three things He has reserved for Himself—to govern, to judge, and to glory. No one has a right to judge or to rule or to have sovereignty except God alone, or those whom He has commissioned with it, those through whom, as His servants, He maintains His rule. In the same way, no man may exercise judgment over another, or become angry at him and punish him, unless he has the office to do so on God's behalf. For this is not a right innate in men, but one given by God. These are the two things that He names here: "the kingdom," that is, the sovereignty by which all authority is His; and then "the power," that is, the consequence of His authority, its execution, by which He can punish, subject the wicked to Himself, and protect the pious. For he who punishes is doing so in God's stead; all administering of justice, all protecting and preserving, is derived from His power. Therefore no one should wreak vengeance or exact punishment on his own; for it does not lie within his official capacity or ability, and it does not do any good either. As He says (Rom. 12:19): "Vengeance is

Mine, I will repay"; and elsewhere He threatens (Matt. 26:52): "All who take the sword for vengeance will be punished by the sword."

In the same way "the glory," or honor or praise, belongs only to God. No one may boast of anything, his wisdom or holiness or ability, except through Him and from Him. When I honor a king or a prince and call him "gracious lord" or bend my knee before him, I am not doing this to him on account of his own person but on account of God, to one who is sitting in majesty in God's stead. It is the same when I show honor to my father and mother or to those who are in their stead. I am not doing this to a human being but to a divine office, and I am honoring God in them. Wherever there is authority and power, therefore, the glory and the praise belong to Him. And so His kingdom, power, and glory prevail throughout the world. It is He alone that is ruling, punishing, and being glorified in the divine offices and stations, like those of father, mother, master, judge, prince, king, and emperor. . . . That is why the petitions for His name, His kingdom, and His will are foremost here; for they alone must prevail, and all other names, kingdoms, powers, and wills must be shattered. Thus we acknowledge that He is supreme in all three of these areas, but that the others are His instruments, by which He acts to accomplish these things.

3. "BLESSED ARE..."

On Matthew 5:2–12

Blessed are the spiritually poor, for theirs is the kingdom of heaven. (5:3)

[Christ] does not come like Moses or a teacher of the Law, with demands, threats, and terrors, but in a very friendly way, with enticements, allurements, and pleasant promises. In fact, if it were not for this report which has preserved for us all the first dear words that the Lord Christ preached, curiosity would drive and impel everyone to run all the way to Jerusalem, or even to the end of the world, just to hear one word of it. You would find plenty of money to build such a road well! And everyone would proudly boast that he had heard or read the very word that the Lord Christ had preached. How wonderfully happy the man would seem who succeeded in this! That is exactly how it would really be if we had none of this in written form, even though there might be a great deal written by others. Everyone would say: "Yes, I hear what St. Paul and His other apostles have taught, but I would much rather hear what He Himself spoke and preached."

But now since it is so common that everyone has it written in a book and can read it every day, no one thinks of it as anything special or precious. Yes, we grow sated and neglect it, as if it had been spoken by some shoemaker rather than the High Majesty of heaven. Therefore it is in punishment for our ingratitude and neglect that we get so little out of it and never feel nor taste what a treasure, power, and might there is in the words of Christ. But whoever has the grace to recognize it as the Word of God rather than the word of man, will also think of it more highly and dearly, and will never grow sick and tired of it.

. . . Christ opens His mouth here and says that something is necessary other than the possession of enough on earth; as if He were to say: "My dear disciples, when you come to preach among the people, you will find out that this is their teaching and belief: 'Whoever is rich or powerful is completely blessed; on the other hand, whoever is poor and miserable is rejected and condemned before God.' " The Jews were firmly persuaded that if a man was successful, this was a sign that he had a gracious God, and vice versa. The reason for this was the fact that they had many great promises from God regarding the temporal, physical goods that He would grant to the pious. They counted upon these, in the opinion that if they had this, they were right with Him. The Book of Job is addressed to this theory. His friends argue and dispute with him about this and insist that he is being punished this way because of some great sin he must have knowingly committed against God. Therefore he ought to admit it, be converted, and become pious, that God might lift the punishment from him.

At the outset, therefore, it was necessary for His sermon to overthrow this delusion and to tear it out of their hearts as one of the greatest obstacles to faith and a great support for the idol Mammon in their heart. Such a doctrine could have no other consequence than to make people greedy, so that everyone would be interested only in amassing plenty and in having a good time, without need or trouble. And everyone would have to conclude: "If that man is blessed who succeeds and has plenty, I must see to it that I do not fall behind."

This is still what the whole world believes today. . . . [It] is the greatest and most universal belief or religion on earth. On it all men depend according to their flesh and blood, and they cannot regard anything else as blessedness. That is why He preaches a totally new sermon here for the Christians: If they are a failure, if they have to suffer poverty and do without riches, power, honor, and good days, they will still be blessed and have not a temporal reward, but a different, eternal one; they will have enough in the kingdom of heaven.

But you say: "What? Must all Christians, then, be poor? Dare none of them have money, property, popularity, power, and the like? What are the rich to do, people like princes, lords, and kings? Must they surrender all their property and honor, or buy the kingdom of heaven from the poor, as some have taught?" Answer: No. It does not say that whoever wants to have the kingdom of heaven must buy it from the poor, but that he must be poor himself and be found among the poor. It is put clearly and candidly, "Blessed are the poor." Yet the little word "spiritually" is added, so that nothing is accomplished when someone is physically poor and has no money or goods. Having money, property, land, and retinue outwardly is not wrong in itself. It is God's gift and ordinance. No one is blessed, therefore, because he is a beggar and owns nothing of his own. The command is to be "spiritually poor."
... Christ is not dealing here at all with the secular realm and order, but wants to discuss only the spiritual—how to live before God, above and beyond the external. ...

So be poor or rich physically and externally, as it is granted to you—God does not ask about this—

and know that before God, in his heart, everyone must be spiritually poor. That is, he must not set his confidence, comfort, and trust on temporal goods, nor hang his heart upon them and make Mammon his idol. David was an outstanding king, and he really had his wallet and treasury full of money, his barns full of grain, his land full of all kinds of goods and provisions. In spite of all this he had to be a poor beggar spiritually, as he sings of himself (Ps. 39:12): "I am poor, and a guest in the land, like all my fathers." Look at the king, sitting amid such possessions, a lord over land and people; yet he does not dare to call himself anything but a guest or a pilgrim, one who walks around on the street because he has no place to stay. This is truly a heart that does not tie itself to property and riches; but though it has, it behaves as if it had nothing, as St. Paul boasts of the Christians (2 Cor. 6:10): "As poor, yet making many rich; as having nothing, and yet possessing everything."

All this is intended to say that while we live here, we should use all temporal goods and physical necessities, the way a guest does in a strange place, where he stays overnight and leaves in the morning. He needs no more than bed and board and dare not say: "This is mine, here I will stay." Nor dare he take possession of the property as though it belonged to him by right; otherwise he would soon hear the host say to him: "My friend, don't you know that you are a guest here? Go back where you belong." That is the way it is here, too. The temporal goods you have, God has given to you for this life. . . . You should not fasten or hang your heart on them as though you were going to live forever. You should always go on and consider another, higher, and better treasure, which is your own and which will last forever. . . .

Then, too, a man is called "rich" in Scripture, even though he does not have any money or property, if he scrambles and scratches for them and can never get enough of them. These are the very ones whom the Gospel calls "rich bellies," who in the midst of great wealth have the very least and are never satisfied with what God grants them. That is so because the Gospel looks into the heart, which is crammed full of money and property, and evaluates on the basis of this, though there may be nothing in the wallet or the treasury. On the other hand, it also calls a man "poor" according to the condition of his heart, though he may have his treasury, house, and hearth full. Thus the Christian faith goes straight ahead. It looks at neither poverty nor riches, but only at the condition of the heart. If there is a greedy belly there, the man is called "spiritually rich"; on the other hand, he is called "spiritually poor" if he does not depend upon these things and can empty his heart of them. As Christ says elsewhere (Matt. 19:29): "He who forsakes houses, land, children, or wife, will receive a hundredfold, and besides he will inherit eternal life." By this He seeks to rescue their hearts from regarding property as their treasure, and to comfort His own who must forsake it; even in this life they will receive more than they leave behind.

We are not to run away from property, house, home, wife, and children, wandering around the countryside as a burden to other people. . . . [Instead, this] is what it means: In our heart we should be able to leave house and home, wife and children. Even though we continue to live among them, eating with them and serving them out of love, as God has commanded, still we should be able, if necessary, to give them up at any time for God's sake. If you are able to do this, you have forsaken everything, in the sense that your heart is not taken captive but remains pure of greed and of dependence, trust, and confidence in anything. A rich man may properly be called "spiritually poor" without discarding his possessions. But when the necessity arises, then let him do so in God's name, not because he would like to get away from wife and children, house and home, but because, as long as God wills it, he would rather keep them and serve Him thereby, yet is also willing to let Him take them back.

So you see what it means to be "poor" spiritually and before God, to have nothing spiritually and to forsake everything. Now look at the promise which Christ appends when He says, "For of such is the kingdom of heaven." This is certainly a great, wonderful, and glorious promise. Because we are willing to be poor here and pay no attention to temporal goods, we are to have a beautiful, glorious, great, and eternal possession in heaven. And because you have given up a crumb, which you still may use as long and as much as you can have it, you are to receive a crown, to be a citizen and a lord in heaven. This would stir us if we really wanted to be Christians and if we believed that His words are true. But no one cares who is saying this, much less what He is saying. They let it go in one ear and out the other, so that no one troubles himself about it or takes it to heart.

With these words He shows that no one can understand this unless he is already a real Christian. This point and all the rest that follow are purely fruits of faith, which the Holy Spirit Himself must create in the heart. Where there is no faith, there the kingdom of heaven also will remain outside; nor will spiritual poverty, meekness, and the like follow, but there will remain only scratching and scraping, quarrels and riots over temporal goods. Therefore it is all over for such worldly hearts, so that they never learn or experience what spiritual poverty is, and neither believe nor care what He says and promises about the kingdom of heaven.

. . . This sermon does the world no good and accomplishes nothing for it. The world stubbornly insists upon being right. It refuses to believe a thing, but must have it before its very eyes and hold it in its hand, saying, "A bird in the hand is worth two in the bush." Therefore Christ also lets them go. He does not want to force anyone or drag him in by the hair. But He gives His faithful advice to all who will let Him advise them, and He holds before us the dearest promises. If you want it, you have peace and quiet in your heart here, and hereafter whatever your heart desires forever. If you do not want it, have your own way, and rather have sorrow and misfortune both here and hereafter. For we see and experience that everything depends upon being content and not clinging to temporal goods. There are many people whose heart God can fill so that they may have only a morsel of bread and yet are cheerful and more content than any prince or king. In brief, such a person is a rich lord and emperor, and he need have no worry, trouble, or sorrow. This is the first point of this sermon: Whoever wants to have enough here and hereafter, let him see to it that he is not greedy or grasping. Let him accept and use what God gives him, and live by his labor in faith. Then he will have Paradise and even the kingdom of heaven here, as St. Paul also says (1 Tim. 4:8): "Godliness is of value in every way, as it holds promise for the present life and also for the life to come."

Blessed are those who mourn, for they shall be comforted. (5:4)

He began this sermon against the doctrine and belief of the whole world [which] even at its best . . . sticks to the delusion that it is well off if it just has property, popularity, and its Mammon here, and which serves God only for this purpose. In the same way He now continues, overturning even what they thought was the best and most blessed life on earth, one in which a person would attain to good and quiet days and would not have to endure discomfort, as Psalm 73:5 describes it: "They are not in trouble as other men are; they are not stricken like other men."

For that is the highest thing that men want, to have joy and happiness and to be without trouble. Now Christ turns the page and says exactly the opposite; He calls "blessed" those who sorrow and mourn. Thus throughout, all these statements are aimed and directed against the world's way of thinking, the way it would like to have things. It does not want to endure hunger, trouble, dishonor, unpopularity, injustice, and violence; and it calls "blessed" those who can avoid all these things.

So He wants to say here that there must be another life than the life of their quests and thoughts, and that a Christian must count on sorrow and mourning in the world. Whoever does not want to do this may have a good time here and live to his heart's desire, but hereafter he will have to mourn forever. As He says (Luke 6:25): "Woe unto you that laugh and have a good time now! For you shall have to mourn and weep." This is how it went with the rich man in Luke 16. He lived luxuriously and joyfully all his life, decked out in expensive silk and purple. He thought he was a great saint and well off in the sight of God because He had given him so much property. Meanwhile he let poor Lazarus lie before his door daily, full of sores, in hunger and trouble and great misery. But what kind of judgment did he finally hear when he was lying in hell? "Remember that in your lifetime you received good things, but Lazarus evil things. Therefore you are now in anguish, but he is comforted" (Luke 16:25).

See, this is the same text as: "Blessed are those who mourn, for they shall be comforted," which is as much as saying, "Those who seek and have nothing but joy and fun here shall weep and howl forever."

You may ask again: "What are we to do, then? Is everyone to be damned who laughs, sings, dances, dresses well, eats, and drinks? After all, we read about kings and saints who were cheerful and lived well. Paul is an especially wonderful saint; he wants us to be cheerful all the time (Phil. 4:4), and he says (Rom. 12:15): 'Rejoice with those who rejoice,' and again: 'Weep with those who weep.' That sounds contradictory, to be joyful all the time and yet to weep and mourn with others."

Answer: I said before that having riches is not sinful, nor is it forbidden. So also being joyful, eating and drinking well, is not sinful or damnable; nor is having honor and a good name. Still I am supposed to be "blessed" if I do not have these things or can do without them, and instead suffer poverty, misery, shame, and persecution. So both of these things are here and must be—being sad and being happy, eating and going hungry, as Paul boasts about himself (Phil. 4:11, 12): "I have learned the art, wherever I am, to be content. I know how to be abased, and I know how to abound; in any and all circumstances I have learned the secret of facing plenty and hunger, abundance and want." And in 2 Corinthians 6:8-10: "In honor and dishonor, in ill repute and good repute; as dying, and, behold, we live; as sorrowful, yet always rejoicing."

So this is what it means: A man is called "spiritually poor," not because he has no money or anything of his own, but because he does not covet it or set his comfort and trust upon it as though it were his kingdom of heaven. So also a man is said to "mourn and be sorrowful"—not if his head is always drooping and his face is always sour and never smiling; but if he does not depend upon having a good time and living it up, the way the world does, which yearns for nothing but having sheer joy and fun here, revels in it, and neither thinks nor cares about the state of God or men. . . .

Therefore mourning and sorrow are not a rare plant among Christians, in spite of outward appearances. They would like to be joyful in Christ, outwardly, too, as much as they can. Daily, whenever they look at the world, they must see and feel in their heart so much wickedness, arrogance, contempt, and blasphemy of God and His Word, so much sorrow and sadness, which the devil causes in both the spiritual and the secular realm. Therefore they cannot have many joyful thoughts, and their spiritual joy is very weak. If they were to look at this continually and did not turn their eyes away from time to time, they could not be happy for a moment. It is bad enough that this really happens oftener than they would like, so that they do not have to go out looking for it.

Therefore simply begin to be a Christian, and

you will soon find out what it means to mourn and be sorrowful. If you can do nothing else, then get married, settle down, and make a living in faith. Love the Word of God, and do what is required of you in your station. Then you will experience, both from your neighbors and in your own household, that things will not go as you might wish. You will be hindered and hemmed in on every side, so that you will suffer enough and see enough to make your heart sad. . . .

Because the world does not want to have such mourning and sorrow, it seeks out those stations and ways of life where it can have fun and does not have to suffer anything from anyone. . . . It cannot stand the idea that [it] should serve other people with nothing but care, toil, and trouble, and get nothing as a reward for this but ingratitude, contempt, and other malicious treatment. Therefore, when things do not go with it as it wishes and one person looks at another with a sour face, all they can do is to batter things with cursing and swearing, and with their fists, too, and be ready to put up property and reputation, land and servants. But God arranges things so that they still cannot get off too easily, without seeing or suffering any trouble at all. What He gives them as a reward for not wanting to suffer is this: they still have to suffer, but by their anger and impatience they make it twice as great and difficult, and without finding any comfort or a good conscience. The Christians have the advantage that though they mourn, too, they shall be comforted and be blessed both here and hereafter. . . .

Those who mourn this way are entitled to have fun and to take it wherever they can so that they do not completely collapse for sorrow. Christ also adds these words and promises this consolation so that they do not despair in their sorrow nor let the joy of their heart be taken away and extinguished altogether, but mix this mourning with comfort and refreshment. Otherwise, if they never had any comfort or joy, they would have to languish and wither away. No man can stand continual mourning. It sucks out the very strength and savor of the body, as the wise man says (Ecclus. 30:25): "Sadness has killed many people"; and again (Prov. 17:22): "A downcast spirit dries up the marrow in the bones." Therefore we should not neglect this but should command and urge such people to have a good time once in a while if possible, or at least to temper their sorrow and forget it for a while.

Thus Christ does not want to urge continual mourning and sorrow. He wants to warn against those who seek to escape all mourning and to have nothing but fun and all their comfort here. And He wants to teach His Christians, when things go badly for them and they have to mourn, to know that it is God's good pleasure and to make it theirs as well, not to curse or rage or despair as though their God did not want to be gracious. When this happens, the bitter draft should be mixed and made milder with honey and sugar. He promises here that this is pleasing to Him; and He calls them "blessed," comforting them here, and hereafter taking the sorrow away from them completely. Therefore say good-by to the world and to all those who harm us, in the name of their lord, the devil. And let us sing this song and be joyful in the name of God and Christ. Their outcome will surely not be the one they want. Now they take pleasure in our misfortune and do much to harm us. Still we take heart, and we shall live to see that at the last they will have to howl and weep when we are comforted and happy.

Blessed are the meek, for they shall inherit the earth. (5:5)

This statement fits the first one well, when He said: "Blessed are the spiritually poor." For as He promises the kingdom of heaven and an eternal possession there, so here He also adds a promise about this temporal life and about possessions here on earth. But how does being poor harmonize with inheriting the land? It might seem that the preacher has forgotten how He began. Whoever is to inherit land and possessions cannot be poor. By "inheriting the land" here and having all sorts of possessions here on earth, He does not mean that everyone is to inherit a whole country; otherwise God would have to create more worlds. But God confers possessions upon everyone in such a way that He gives a man wife, children, cattle, house, and home, and whatever pertains to these, so that he can stay on the land where he lives and have dominion over his possessions. This is the way Scripture customarily speaks, as Psalm 37 says several times (Ps. 37:34): "Those who wait for the Lord will inherit the land"; and again (Ps. 37:22): "His blessed ones inherit the land." Therefore He adds His own gloss here: to be "spiritually poor," as He used the expression before, does not mean to be a beggar or to discard money and possessions. For here He tells them to live and remain in the land and to manage earthly possessions. . . .

What does it mean, then, to be meek? From the outset here you must realize that Christ is not speaking at all about the government and its work, whose property it is not to be meek . . . for the punishment of those who do wrong (1 Peter 2:14), and to wreak a vengeance and a wrath that are called the vengeance and wrath of God. He is only talking about how individuals are to live in relation to others, apart from official position and authority —how father and mother are to live, not in relation to their children nor in their official capacity as father and mother, but in relation to those for whom they are not father and mother, like neighbors and other people. I have often said that we must sharply distinguish between these two, the office and the person. The man who is called Hans or Martin is a man quite different from the one who is called elector or doctor or preacher. Here we have two different persons in one man. The one is that in which we are created and born, according to which we are all alike—man or woman or child, young or old. But once we are born, God adorns and dresses you up as another person. He makes you a child and me a father, one a master and another a servant, one a prince and another a citizen. Then this one is called a divine person, one who holds a divine office and goes about clothed in its dignity —not simply Hans or Nick, but the Prince of Saxony, father, or master. He is not talking about this person here, letting it alone in its own office and rule, as He has ordained it. He is talking merely about how each individual, natural person is to behave in relation to others. . . .

You see, then, that here Christ is rebuking those crazy saints who think that everyone is master of the whole world and is entitled to be delivered from all suffering, to roar and bluster and violently to defend his property. And He teaches us that whoever wants to rule and possess his property, his possessions, house, and home in peace, must be meek, so that he may overlook things and act reasonably, putting up with just as much as he possibly can. It is inevitable that your neighbor will sometimes do you injury or harm, either accidentally or maliciously. If he did it accidentally, you do not improve the situation by refusing or being unable to endure anything. If he did it maliciously, you only irritate him by your violent scratching and pounding; meanwhile he is laughing at you and enjoying the fact that he is baiting and troubling you, so that you still cannot have any peace or quietly enjoy what is yours.

So select one of the two, whichever you prefer: either to live in human society with meekness and patience and to hold on to what you have with peace and a good conscience; or boisterously and blusterously to lose what is yours, and to have no peace besides. There stands the decree: "The meek shall inherit the earth." Just take a look for yourself at the queer characters who are always arguing and squabbling about property and other things. They refuse to give in to anybody, but insist on rushing everything through headlong, regardless of whether their quarreling and squabbling costs them more than they could ever gain. Ultimately they lose their land and servants, house and home, and get unrest and a bad conscience thrown in. And God adds His blessing to it, saying: "Do not be meek, then, so that you may not keep your precious land, nor enjoy your morsel in peace."

But if you want to do right and have rest, let your neighbor's malice and viciousness smother and burn itself out. . . . Do you have a government? Then register a complaint, and let it see to it. The government has the charge not to permit the harsh oppression of the innocent. God will also overrule so that His Word and ordinance may abide and you may inherit the land according to this promise. Thus you will have rest and God's blessing, but your neighbor will have unrest together with God's displeasure and curse. This sermon is intended only for those who are Christians, who believe and know that they have their treasure in heaven, where it is secure for them and cannot be taken away. Hence they must have enough here, too, even though they do not have treasuries and pockets full of yellow guldens. Since you know this, why let your joy be disturbed and taken away? Why cause yourself disquiet and rob yourself of this magnificent promise?

See now that you have three points with three rich promises. Whoever is a Christian must have enough of both the temporal and the eternal, though here he must suffer much both outwardly and inwardly, in the heart. On the other hand, because the worldlings refuse to endure poverty or trouble or violence, they neither have the kingdom of heaven nor enjoy temporal goods peacefully and quietly. . . .

Blessed are those who hunger and thirst for righteousness, for they shall be satisfied. (5:6)

"Righteousness" in this passage must not be taken in the sense of that principal Christian righteousness by which a person becomes pious and acceptable to God. . . . These eight items are nothing but instruction about the fruits and good works of a Christian. Before these must come faith, as the tree and chief part or summary of a man's righteousness and blessedness, without any work or merit of his; out of which faith these items all must grow and follow. Therefore take this in the sense of the outward righteousness before the world, which we maintain in our relations with each other. Thus the short and simple meaning of these words is this: "That man is righteous and blessed who continually works and strives with all his might to promote the general welfare and the proper behavior of everyone and who helps to maintain and support this by word and deed, by precept and example."

Now, this is also a precious point, embracing very many good works, but by no means a common thing. Let me illustrate with an example. If a preacher wants to qualify under this point, he must be ready to instruct and help everyone to perform his assigned task properly and to do what it requires. And when he sees that something is missing and things are not going right, he should be on hand to warn, rebuke, and correct by whatever method or means he can. . . . In this way the right thing is done on both sides. Now, where there are people who earnestly take it upon themselves to do right gladly and to be found engaged in the right works and ways—such people "hunger and thirst for righteousness." If this were the situation, there would be no rascality or injustice, but sheer righteousness and blessedness on earth. What is the righteousness of the world except that in his station everyone should do his duty? That means that the rights of every station should be respected—those of the man, the woman, the child, the manservant, and the maid in the household, the citizen of the city in the land. And it is all contained in this, that those who are charged with overseeing and ruling other people should execute this office diligently, carefully, and faithfully, and that the others should also render their due service and obedience to them faithfully and willingly.

It is not by accident that He uses the term "hunger and thirst for righteousness." By it He intends to point out that this requires great earnestness, longing, eagerness, and unceasing diligence and that where this hunger and thirst is lacking, everything will fail. The reason is that there are too many great hindrances. They come from the devil, who is blocking and barricading the way everywhere. They also come from the world—that is, his children—which is so wicked that it cannot stand a pious man who wants to do right himself or to help other people do so, but plagues him in every way, that he finally becomes tired and perplexed over the whole business. It is painful to see how shamefully people behave, and to get no reward for pure kindness except ingratitude, contempt, hate, and persecution. . . .

. . . Anyone who tries to preach or rule in such a way that he lets himself become tired and impatient and be chased into a corner will not be of much help to other people. The command to you is not to crawl into a corner or into the desert, but to run out, if that is where you have been, and to offer your hands and your feet and your whole body, and to wager everything you have and can do. You should be the kind of man who is firm in the face of firmness, who will not let himself be frightened off or dumbfounded or overcome by the world's ingratitude or malice, who will always hold on and push with all the might he can summon. In short, the ministry requires a hunger and thirst for righteousness that can never be curbed or stopped or sated, one that looks for nothing and cares for nothing except the accomplishment and maintenance of the right, despising everything that hinders this end. If you cannot make the world completely pious, then do what you can. It is enough that you have done your duty and have helped a few, even if there be only one or two. If others will not follow, then in God's name let them go. You must not run away on account of the wicked, but rather conclude: "I did not undertake this for their sakes, and I shall not drop it for their sakes. Eventually some of them might come around; at least there might be fewer of them, and they may improve a little."

Here you have a comforting and certain promise, with which Christ allures and attracts His Christians: "Those who hunger and thirst for righteousness shall be filled." That is, they will be recompensed for their hunger and thirst by seeing that their work was not in vain and that at last a little flock has been brought around who have been helped. Although things are not going now as they would like and they have almost despaired over it, all this will become manifest, not only here on earth, but even more in the life hereafter, when everyone will see what sort of fruit such people have brought by their diligence and perseverance. . . .

Blessed are the merciful, for they shall obtain mercy. (5:7)

This is also an outstanding fruit of faith, and it follows well upon what went before. Anyone who is supposed to help other people and to contribute to the common weal and success should also be kind and merciful. He should not immediately raise a rumpus and start a riot if something is missing or if things do not go as they should, as long as there is still some hope for improvement. One of the virtues of counterfeit sanctity is that it cannot have pity or mercy for the frail and weak, but insists on the strictest enforcement and the purest selection; as soon as there is even a minor flaw, all mercy is gone, and there is nothing but fuming and fury. St. Gregory also teaches us how to recognize this when he says: "True justice shows mercy, but false justice shows indignation." True holiness is merciful and sympathetic, but all that false holiness can do is to rage and fume. Yet it does so, as they boast, "out of zeal for justice"; that is, it is done through love and zeal for righteousness. . . .

. . . If a man deals with his neighbor in an effort

to help and correct him in his station and way of life, he should still take care to be merciful and to forgive. In this way people will see that your aim really is righteousness and not the gratification of your own malice and anger; for you are righteous enough to deal in a friendly and gentle manner with the man who is willing to forsake his unrighteousness and improve himself, and you tolerate and endure his fault or weakness until he comes around. But if you try all this and find no hope for improvement, then you may give him up and turn him over to those whose duty it is to punish.

Now, this is the one aspect of mercy, that one gladly forgives the sinful and the frail. The other is to do good also to those who are outwardly poor or in need of help; on the basis of Matthew 25:35 ff. we call these "works of mercy." . . .

. . . The only pupils [this message] finds are those who already cling to Christ and believe in Him. They know of no holiness of their own. On the basis of the preceding items they are poor, miserable, meek, really hungry and thirsty; they are inclined not to despise anyone, but to assume and to sympathize with the need of everyone else. To them applies the comforting promise: "It is well with you who are merciful. For you will find pure mercy in turn, both here and hereafter, and a mercy which inexpressibly surpasses all human kindness and mercy." There is no comparison between our mercy and God's, nor between our possessions and the eternal possessions in the kingdom of heaven. So pleased is He with our kindness to our neighbor that for one pfennig He promises us a hundred thousand guldens if we have need of them, and for a drink of water, the kingdom of heaven (Matt. 10:42).

Now, if anyone will not let himself be moved by this wonderful and comforting promise, let him turn the page and hear another judgment: "Woe and curses upon the unmerciful, for no mercy shall be shown to them." . . .

St. James also says (James 2:13): "Judgment without mercy will be spoken over the one who has shown no mercy." At the Last Day, therefore, Christ will also cite this lack of mercy as the worst injury done to Him, whatever we have done out of a lack of mercy. He Himself will utter the curse (Matt. 25:41, 42): "I was hungry and thirsty, and you gave Me no food, you gave Me no drink. Depart from Me, therefore, you cursed, into eternal hell-fire." . . .

Blessed are those of a pure heart, for they shall see God. (5:8)

What is meant by a "pure heart" is this: one that is watching and pondering what God says and replacing its own ideas with the Word of God. This alone is pure before God, yes, purity itself, which purifies everything that it includes and touches. Therefore, though a common laborer, a shoemaker, or a blacksmith may be dirty and sooty or may smell because he is covered with dirt and pitch, still he may sit at home and think: "My God has made me a man. He has given me my house, wife, and child and has commanded me to love them and to support them with my work." Note that he is pondering the Word of God in his heart; and though he stinks outwardly, inwardly he is pure incense before God. But if he attains the highest purity so that he also takes hold of the Gospel and believes in Christ—without this, that purity is impossible—then he is pure completely, inwardly in his heart toward God and outwardly toward everything under him on earth. Then everything he is and does, his walking, standing, eating, and drinking, is pure for him; and nothing can make him impure. So it is when he looks at his own wife or fondles her, as the patriarch Isaac did (Gen. 26:8). . . . For here he has the Word of God, and he knows that God has given her to him. But if he were to desert his wife and take up another, or neglect his job or duty to harm or bother other people, he would no longer be pure; for that would be contrary to God's commandment.

But so long as he sticks to these two—namely, the Word of faith toward God, which purifies the heart, and the Word of understanding, which teaches him what he is to do toward his neighbor . . . —everything is pure for him, even if with his hands and the rest of his body he handles nothing but dirt. If a poor housemaid does her duty and is a Christian in addition, then before God in heaven she is a lovely and pure beauty, one that all the angels admire and love to look at. . . .

So you see that everything depends on the Word of God. Whatever is included in that and goes in accordance with it, must be called clean, pure, and white as snow before both God and man. Therefore Paul says (Titus 1:15): "To the pure all things are pure"; and again: "To the corrupt and unbelieving nothing is pure." Why is this so? Because both their minds and their consciences are impure. How does this happen? Because "they profess to know God, but with their deeds they deny it" (Titus 1:16). . . .

. . . Whatever God does and ordains must be pure and good. For He makes nothing impure, and He consecrates everything through the Word which He has attached to every station and creature.

Therefore be on guard against all your own ideas if you want to be pure before God. See to it that your heart is founded and fastened on the Word of

God. Then you will be purer than all the Carthusians and saints in the world. When I was young, people used to take pride in this proverb: "Enjoy being alone, and your heart will stay pure." In support of it they would cite a quotation from St. Bernard, who said that whenever he was among people, he defiled himself. In the lives of the fathers we read about a hermit who would not let anyone come near him or talk to him, because, he said: "The angels cannot come to anyone who moves around in human society." We also read about two others, who would not let their mother see them. She kept watch, and once she caught them. Immediately they closed the door and let her stand outside for a long time crying; finally they persuaded her to go away and to wait until they would see each other in the life hereafter. . . .

[Instead of seeking pureness through such a solitary life, let it be] where God has put it, in a heart that clings to God's Word and that regards its tasks and every creature on the basis of it. Then the chief purity, that of faith toward God, will also manifest itself outwardly in this life; and everything will proceed from obedience to the Word and command of God, regardless of whether it is physically clean or unclean. I spoke earlier of a judge who has to condemn a man to death, who thus sheds blood and defiles himself with it. A monk would regard this as an abominably impure act, but Scripture says it is the service of God. In Rom. 13:4 Paul calls the government, which bears the sword, "God's servant." This is not its work and command, but His, which He imposes on it and demands from it.

Now you have the meaning of "pure heart": it is one that functions completely on the basis of the pure Word of God. What is their reward, what does He promise to them? It is this: "They shall see God." A wonderful title and an excellent treasure! But what does it mean to "see God"? Here again the monks have their own dreams. To them it means sitting in a cell and elevating your thoughts heavenward, leading a "contemplative life," as they call it in the many books they have written about it. . . . But this is what it is: if you have a true faith that Christ is your Savior, then you see immediately that you have a gracious God. For faith leads you up and opens up the heart and will of God for you. There you see sheer, superabundant grace and love. That is exactly what it means "to see God," not with physical eyes, with which no one can see Him in this life, but with faith, which sees His fatherly, friendly heart, where there is no anger or displeasure. Anyone who regards Him as angry is not seeing Him correctly, but has pulled down a curtain and cover, more, a dark cloud over His face. But in Scriptural language "to see His face" means to recognize Him correctly as a gracious and faithful Father, on whom you can depend for every good thing. This happens only through faith in Christ.

Therefore, if according to God's Word and command you live in your station with your husband, wife, child, neighbor, or friend, you can see God's intention in these things; and you can come to the conclusion that they please Him, since this is not your own dream, but His Word and command, which never deludes or deceives us. It is a wonderful thing, a treasure beyond every thought or wish, to know that you are standing and living in the right relation to God. In this way not only can your heart take comfort and pride in the assurance of His grace, but you can know that your outward conduct and behavior is pleasing to Him. From this it follows that cheerfully and heartily you can do and suffer anything, without letting it make you fearful or despondent. None of this is possible for those who lack this faith and pure heart, guided only by God's Word.

. . . No one can boast that in all his life and activity he has ever seen God. Or if in his pride someone glorifies such works and thinks that God must be well disposed to them and reward him for them, he is not seeing God but the devil in place of God. There is no word of God to support him; it is all the invention of men, grown up in their own hearts. That is why it can never assure or pacify any heart, but remain hidden by pride until it comes to its final gasps, when it all disappears and brings on despair, so that one never gets around to seeing the face of God. But anyone who takes hold of the Word of God and who remains in faith can take his stand before God and look at Him as his gracious Father. He does not have to be afraid that He is standing behind him with a club, and he is sure that He is looking at him and smiling graciously, together with all the angels and saints in heaven.

You see, that is what Christ means by this statement, that only those who have such a pure heart see God. By this He cuts off and puts aside every other kind of purity. Where this kind is absent, everything else in a man may be pure; but it is worth nothing before God, and he can never see God. Where the heart is pure, on the other hand, everything is pure; and it does not matter if outwardly everything is impure, yes, if the body is full of sores, scabs, and leprosy.

Blessed are the peacemakers, for they shall be called the children of God. (5:9)

With an excellent title and wonderful praise the Lord here honors those who do their best to try to make peace, not only in their own lives but also among other people, who try to settle ugly and involved issues, who endure squabbling and try to avoid and prevent war and bloodshed. This is a great virtue, too, but one that is very rare in the world and among the counterfeit saints. . . . If a prince loses his temper, he immediately thinks he has to start a war. Then he inflames and incites everyone, until there has been so much war and bloodshed that he regrets it and gives a few thousand guldens for the souls that were killed. These are bloodhounds, and that is what they remain. They cannot rest until they have taken revenge and spent their anger, until they have dragged their land and people into misery and sorrow. Yet they claim to bear the title "Christian princes" and to have a just cause.

You need more to start a war than having a just cause. As we have said, this does not prohibit the waging of war; for Christ has no intention here of taking anything away from the government and its official authority, but is only teaching individuals who want to lead a Christian life. Still it is not right for a prince to make up his mind to go to war against his neighbor, even though, I say, he has a just cause and his neighbor is in the wrong. The command is: "Blessed are the peacemakers." Therefore anyone who claims to be a Christian and a child of God, not only does not start war or unrest; but he also gives help and counsel on the side of peace wherever he can, even though there may have been a just and adequate cause for going to war. It is sad enough if one has tried everything and nothing helps, and then he has to defend himself, to protect his land and people. Therefore not "Christians" but "children of the devil" is the name for those quarrelsome young noblemen who immediately draw and unsheathe their sword on account of one word. Even worse are the ones that are now persecuting the Gospel and ordering the burning and murder of innocent preachers of the Gospel, who have done them no harm but only good and have served them with body and soul. We are not talking about these right now, but only about those who claim that they are in the right and have a just cause and think that as high and princely personages they ought not to suffer, even though other people do.

This also means that if you are the victim of injustice and violence, you have no right to take the advice of your own foolish head and immediately start getting even and hitting back; but you are to think it over, try to bear it and have peace. If that is impossible and you cannot stand it, you have law and government in the country, from which you can seek legitimate redress. It is ordained to guard against such things and to punish them. Therefore anyone who does violence to you sins not only against you but also against the government itself; for the order and command to maintain peace was given to the government and not to you. Therefore leave the vengeance and punishment to your judge, who has the command; it is against him that your enemy has done wrong. If you take it upon yourself to wreak vengeance, you do an even greater wrong. You become guilty of the same sin as he who sins against the government and interferes with its duties, and by doing so you invalidate the justice of your own righteous cause. For the proverb says: "The one who strikes back is in the wrong, and striking back makes a quarrel."

Note that this is one demand that Christ makes here in opposition to those who are vengeful and violent. He gives the name "peacemakers," in the first place, to those who help make peace among lands and people, like pious princes, counselors, or jurists, to people in government who hold their rule and reign for the sake of peace; and in the second place, to pious citizens and neighbors, who with their salutary and good tongues adjust, reconcile, and settle quarrels and tensions between husband and wife or between neighbors, brought on by evil and poisonous tongues. Thus St. Augustine boasts that when his mother Monica saw two people at odds, she would always speak the best to both sides. Whatever good she heard about the one, she brought to the other; but whatever evil she heard, that she kept to herself or mitigated as much as possible. In this way she often brought on a reconciliation. This is [in contrast to] the work of those bitter and poisonous brides of the devil, who when they hear a word about another, viciously make it sharper, more pointed, and more bitter against the others, so that sometimes misery and murder are the result.

All this comes from the shameful, demonic filth which naturally clings to us, that everyone enjoys hearing and telling the worst about his neighbor and it tickles him to see a fault in someone else. If a woman were as beautiful as the sun but had one little spot or blemish on her body, you would be expected to forget everything else and to look only for that spot and to talk about it. If a lady were famous for her honor and virtue, still some poisonous tongue would come along and say that she had once been seen laughing with some man and defame her in such a way as to eclipse all her praise and honor. These are really poisonous spiders that can suck out nothing but poison from a beautiful, lovely rose, ruining both the flower and the nectar, while a little bee sucks out nothing but honey, leaving the roses unharmed. That is the way some people act. All they can notice about other people are the faults or impurities which they can denounce, but what is good about them they do not see. People have many virtues which the devil cannot destroy, yet he hides or disfigures them to make them invisible. For example, even though a woman may be full of faults and have no other virtue, she is still a creature of God. At least she can carry water and wash clothes. There is no person on earth so bad that he does not have something about him that is praiseworthy. Why is it, then, that we leave the good things out of sight and feast our eyes on the unclean things? It is as though we enjoyed only looking at—if you will pardon the expression—a man's behind, while God Himself has covered the unpresentable parts of the body and, as Paul says (1 Cor. 12:24), has given them "greater honor." . . .

. . . Learn to put the best interpretation on what you hear about your neighbor, or even to conceal it, so that you may establish and preserve peace and harmony. Then you can honorably bear the title "child of God" before the whole world and before the angels in heaven. You should let this honor draw and attract you; in fact, you should chase it to the end of the world, if need be, and gladly surrender everything you have for it. Now you have it offered to you here and spread out in front of you for nothing. There is nothing that you have to do or give for it, except that if you want to be a child of God, you must also show yourself to be one and do your Father's works toward your neighbor. This is what Christ, our Lord, has done for us by reconciling us to the Father, bringing us into His favor, daily representing us, and interceding on our behalf.

You do the same. Be a reconciler and a mediator between your neighbors. Carry the best to both sides; but keep quiet about the bad, which the devil has inspired, or explain it the best way you can. If you come to Margaret, do what is said of Monica, Augustine's mother, and say: "My dear Margaret, why are you so bitter? Surely she does not intend it so badly. All I notice about her is that she would like to be your dear sister." In the same way, if you meet Catherine, do the same thing. Then, as a true child of God, you will have made peace on both sides as far as possible.

But if you will or must talk about an evil deed, do as Christ has taught you. Do not carry it to others, but go to the one who has done it, and admonish him to improve. Do not act ostentatiously when you come and expose the person involved, speaking when you ought to be quiet and being quiet when you ought to speak. This is the first method: You should discuss it between yourself and your neighbor alone (Matt. 18:15). If you must tell it to others, however, when the first method does not work, then tell it to those who have the job of punishing, father and mother, master and mistress, burgomaster and judge. That is the right and proper procedure for removing and punishing a wrong. Otherwise, if you spread it among other people, the person remains unimproved; and the wrong remains unpunished, besides being broadcast by you and by others, so that everyone washes out his mouth with it. Look what a faithful physician does with a sick child. He does not run around among the people and broadcast it; but he goes to the child and examines his pulse or anything else that is necessary, not to gratify his pleasure at the cost of the child, nor to make fun of him, but with the good, honest intention of helping him. So we read about the holy patriarch Joseph in Genesis 37. He was tending the cattle with his brothers, and when he heard an evil report about them, he went and brought it to their father as their superior, whose task it was to investigate and to punish them because they would not listen to him. . . .

Blessed are those who are persecuted for righteousness' sake, for theirs is the kingdom of heaven. (5:10)

I have said earlier that all these items and promises must be understood by faith in reference to things that are neither seen nor heard and that they are not talking about outward appearances. How can the poor and the mourners be said to look outwardly successful and blessed when, in addition, they have to suffer all sorts of persecution—all things that the whole world and our reason calls trouble and that they say should be avoided? Therefore whoever wants to have the blessedness and the possessions that Christ is talking about here, must lift up his heart far above all senses and reason. He must not evaluate himself on the basis of his feelings, but he must argue this way: "If I am poor, then I am not poor. I am poor outwardly, according to the flesh; but before God, in faith, I am rich." Thus when he feels sad, troubled, and worried, he must not use this standard and say that he is not a blessed man. But he must turn himself over and say: "I feel sorrow, misery, and sadness of heart; but still I am blessed, happy, and settled on the basis of the Word of God." The situation in the world is the exact counterpart of this, for those who are called rich and happy are not. Christ calls out His "Woe!" against them and calls them unhappy (Luke 6:24, 25), although it appears that they are well off and having the greatest possible success. Therefore they should lift up their thoughts above the riches and fun which they are having and say: "Yes, I am rich and living in the midst of pure fun. But too bad for me if I have nothing else; for there must certainly be plenty of trouble, misery, and sorrow in all this that will come over me before I feel it or know it." This applies to all these items; every one of them looks different before the world from the way it looks according to these words.

So far we have been treating almost all the elements of a Christian's way of life and the spiritual fruits under these two headings: first, that in his own person he is poor, troubled, miserable, needy, and hungry; second, that in relation to others he is a useful, kind, merciful, and peaceable man, who does nothing but good works. Now He adds the last: how he fares in all this. Although he is full of good works, even toward his enemies and rascals, for all this he must get this reward from the world: he is persecuted and runs the risk of losing his body, his life, and everything.

If you want to be a Christian, therefore, consider this well, lest you be frightened, lose heart, and become impatient. But be cheerful and content, knowing that you are not badly off when this happens to you. He and all the saints had the same experience, as He says a little later. For this reason He issues a warning beforehand to those who want to be Christians, that they should and must suffer persecution. Therefore you may take your choice. You have two ways before you—either to heaven and eternal life or to hell, either with Christ or with the world. But this you must know: if you live in order to have a good time here without persecution, then you will not get to heaven with Christ, and vice versa. In short, you must either surrender Christ and heaven or make up your mind that you are willing to suffer every kind of persecution and torture in the world. Briefly, anyone who wants to have Christ must put in jeopardy his body, life, goods, reputation, and popularity in the world. He dare not let himself be scared off by contempt, ingratitude, or persecution. . . .

. . . It is significant that He should add the phrase: "for righteousness' sake," to show that where this condition is absent, persecution alone will not accomplish this. The devil and wicked people also have to suffer persecution. Rascals often get into each other's hair, and there is no love lost between them. So one murderer persecutes another, and the Turk battles against the Tartar; but this does not make them blessed. This statement applies only to those who are persecuted for righteousness' sake. So also 1 Peter 4:15 says: "Let none of you suffer as a murderer or a thief or a wrongdoer." Therefore bragging and yelling about great suffering is worthless without this condition. . . .

See to it, therefore, that you have a genuine divine cause for whose sake you suffer persecution, and that you are really convinced of it so that your conscience can take a stand and stick by it, even though the whole world should stand up against you. The primary thing is that you grasp the Word of God firmly and surely so that there can be no doubt or hesitation there. Suppose that the Emperor, the bishops, or the princes were to forbid marriage, freedom in the choice of food, the use of both kinds in the Sacrament, and the like, and were to persecute you for these things. Then you would have to see to it that your heart is convinced and persuaded that the Word of God has made these things free and unprohibited, that it even commands us to take them seriously and to stake our lives upon them. Then you can have the confidence to say: "This cause does not belong to me but to Christ, my Lord. For I have not concocted it out of my own head. I have not assumed or begun it on my own or at the advice or suggestion of any man. But it has been brought and announced to me from heaven through the mouth of Christ, who never deludes or deceives me but is Himself sheer Truth and Righteousness. At this Man's Word I will take the risk of suffering, of doing and forsaking whatever I should. All by itself, His Word will accomplish more to comfort and strengthen my heart than the raging and threatening of all the devils and of the world can accomplish to frighten me."

Who cares if a crazy prince or foolish emperor

fumes in his rage and threatens me with sword, fire, or the gallows! Just as long as my Christ is talking dearly to my heart, comforting me with the promises that I am blessed, that I am right with God in heaven, and that all the heavenly host and creation call me blessed. Just let my heart and mind be ready to suffer for the sake of His Word and work. Then why should I let myself be scared by these miserable people, who rage and foam in their hostility to God but suddenly disappear like a puff of smoke or a bubble, as the prophet Isaiah says (Isa. 51:12, 13): "I, I am He that comforts you; who are you that you are afraid of man who dies, of the son of man who is made like grass, and have forgotten the Lord, who made you, who stretched out the heavens and laid the foundations of the earth?" That is to say: "He who comforts you and takes pleasure in you is almighty and eternal. When it is all over with them, He will still be sitting up there, and so will you. Why, then, let the threatening and fuming of a miserable [oppressor] concern you more than this divine comfort and approval? Be grateful to God and happy in your heart that you are worthy of suffering this, as the apostles went forth (Acts 5:41) leaping for joy over the fact that they were disgraced and beaten down."

You see, these words are a great blessing to us if

only we receive them with love and thanks, since we have no shortage of persecution. . . .

So let us be all the more willing and happy to suffer everything. . . . We hear the wonderful and delightful promise here that we shall be well rewarded in heaven and that we should be happy and rejoice over this, as people who do not have to yearn for heaven but already have it. . . . Now tell me whether these simple, short words do not encourage you as much as the whole world can, and provide comfort and joy. . . . We should not listen to them with only *half* an ear, but take them to heart and ponder them.

This applies to persecution with deeds and fists, involving person or property, when Christians are seized and tortured, burned, hanged, and massacred, as happens nowadays and has happened before. There is, in addition, another kind of persecution. It is called defamation, slander, or disgrace, involving our reputation and good name. In this way Christians have to suffer more than others. Now Christ discusses this.

Blessed are you when men revile you and persecute you and utter all kinds of evil against you falsely on My account. (5:11)

This, too, is a great and severe persecution and, as I have said, the real suffering of Christians, that they endure bitter slander and poisonous defamation. Though other people must also suffer persecution, violent and unjust treatment, still men are willing to let them keep their reputation and good name. So this is not yet really Christian suffering, which requires not merely all sorts of tortures and troubles, but more; their good name must be spit upon and slandered, and the world must boast loudly that in murdering the Christians it has executed the worst kind of criminal, whom the earth could no longer carry, and that it has done God the greatest and most acceptable service, as Christ says (John 16:2). Thus no name has ever appeared on earth so slanderous and disreputable as the name "Christian." No nation has ever experienced so much bitter opposition and attack by wicked and poisonous tongues as have the Christians.

. . . Anyone who wants to be a Christian should learn to expect such persecution from poisonous, evil, slanderous tongues, especially when they cannot do anything with their fists. He should let the whole world sharpen its tongue on him, aim at him, sting and bite. Meanwhile he should regard all this with defiant contempt and laughter in God's name, being firmly persuaded, that our cause is the right cause and is God's own cause. . . . [Before] God our heart and conscience are sure that our teaching is right. We are not teaching on the basis of our own brains, reason, or wisdom, or using this to gain advantage, property, or reputation for ourselves before the world. We are preaching only God's Word and praising only His deeds. We praise nothing but the Gospel, Christ, faith, and truly good works, and because we do not suffer for ourselves but suffer everything for the sake of Christ, the Lord. Therefore we will sing it to the end. . . .

Rejoice and be glad, for your reward is great in heaven. (5:12a)

These are really sweet and comforting words. They should gladden and encourage our hearts against all kinds of persecution. Should not the dear Lord's Word and comfort be dearer and more important to us than that which comes from a [vile human]? . . . For I hear my Lord Christ telling me that He is truly delighted, and commanding me to be happy about it. In addition, He promises me such a wonderful reward: the kingdom of heaven shall be mine and everything that Christ has, together with all the saints and all Christendom—in short, such a treasure and comfort that I should not trade it for all the possessions, joy, and music in the whole world, even though all the leaves and all the blades of grass were tongues singing my praises. This is not a Christian calling me "blessed," nor even an angel, but the Lord of all the angels, before whom they and all the creatures must kneel and adore. With all the other creatures, therefore, with the leaves and the grass, they must cheerfully sing and dance in my honor and praise.

. . . If every creature, the leaves and the blades of grass in the forest and the sand on the shore, were all tongues to accuse and destroy them, what would all that be in comparison with a single word of this Man? His voice sounds clear enough to fill heaven and earth and to echo through them, silencing the slobbering coughs and the hoarse scratching of His enemies.

You see, that is how we should learn something about using these words for our benefit. They are not put here for nothing, but were spoken and written for our strengthening and comfort. By them our dear Master and faithful Shepherd, or Bishop, arms us. Then we shall be unafraid and ready to suffer if for His sake [enemies] lay all kinds of torment and trouble upon us in both words and deeds, and we shall despise whatever is offensive to us, even though contrary to our own reason and heart.

For if we cling to our own thoughts and feelings, we are dismayed and hurt to learn that for our service, help, counsel, and kindness to the world and to everyone we should get no thanks except the deepest and bitterest hatred and cursed, poisonous tongues. If flesh and blood were in charge here, it would soon say: "If I am to get nothing else out of this, then let anyone who wants to, stick with the Gospel and be a Christian! . . ."

. . . Here is what it says: "If you do not want to have the Gospel or be a Christian, then go out and take the world's side. Then you will be its friend, and no one will persecute you. But if you want to have the Gospel and Christ, then you must count on having trouble, conflict, and persecution wherever you go." Reason: because the devil cannot bear it otherwise, nor will he stop egging people on against the Gospel, so that all the world is incensed against it. Thus at the present time peasants, city people, nobles, princes, and lords oppose the Gospel from sheer cussedness, and they themselves do not know why.

So this is what I say in reply to these idle talkers and grumblers: "Things neither can nor should run peacefully and smoothly. How could things run smoothly, when the devil is in charge and is a mortal enemy of the Gospel? There is good reason for this, too, since it hurts him in his kingdom, where he can feel it. If he were to let it go ahead unhindered, it would soon be all over and his kingdom would be utterly destroyed. But if he is to resist it and hinder it, he must rally all his art and power and arouse everything in his might against it. . . ."

. . . We are sure that [enemies] cannot accomplish

what they desire until they first topple Christ from heaven and make a liar out of Him, with all that He has said.

For so men persecuted the prophets who were before you. (5:12b)

"When this happens," He wants to say, "you are not alone. Look around, count back to all the holy fathers that ever lived before you, and you will find that their lot was the same. Why should you expect any special treatment? Should He forsake His method for your sake? He had to put up with it when His dear fathers and prophets were persecuted and killed, slandered, and ridiculed by everyone, and made the mockery of the world." As we see from the Scriptures, it had become a common and proverbial expression that if someone wanted to refer to a prophet, he called him a "fool." So in the history of Jehu (2 Kings 9:11), they said of a prophet: "Why did this mad fellow come to you?" And Isaiah shows (Isa. 57:4) that they opened their mouths and put out their tongues against him. But all they accomplished by this was to become a terrible stench and a curse, while the dear prophets and saints have honor, praise, and acclaim throughout the world and are ruling forever with Christ, the Lord. "This is what you should expect for yourselves, too," Christ says, "that you will receive the same reward that they did, a reward more abundant and glorious than you can believe or dare to wish. For you are members of the same company and congregation."

What a dear and wonderful Preacher and faithful Master! He leaves out nothing that will help to strengthen and console, whether it be His Word and promise or the example and testimony of all the saints and of Himself. And all the angels in heaven and all the creatures support this. What more would you want and need? With such comfort, should we not put up with the anger and spite of the world and the devil for His sake? What would we do if we did not have a righteous and divine cause, if we had no splendid sayings and assurances like these and still had to suffer, as other people do who have no comfort? In the world it is impossible to avoid all suffering. And for the sake of the Gospel, as we have said, there must be some suffering; it reinforces the faithful and advances them to their promised comfort, joy, and bliss.